New Aesthetic

New Aesthetic 2

A Collection of Experimental and Independent Type Design

Edited by Leonhard Laupichler & Sophia Brinkgerd

Sorry Press

Human language shows itself in so many artifacts of visual expression. Letters, hieroglyphs, runes and icons—written language can work in many ways. Typography as we understand it today can serve us as a universal, reliable and longevous tool. What if we saw it as a playground? Designing on a molecular basis, questioning the smallest unit of design, we can reinterpret what typography means. Can it be a keepsake from a creative odyssey, a teacher, or simply just an ephemeral servant? "New Aesthetic" challenges typography as a tool in reading culture and in its functional shape—more so seeing letters in their individual appearance as artworks of their own. Independent type design doesn't seek competition, it doesn't seek utter perfection, it tells stories of formal exploration and creates an expressive form of art in itself. The expressive nature of non-traditional, more open typography is a new kind of creative output worth aiming for and worth exploring. Technical perfectionism and a classical understanding of polished shapes are not the main parts of our debate. More so, "New Aesthetic" wants to acknowledge creative processes and see the stories behind them, as well as encourage designers to keep an open attitude towards new forms, styles and systems. There is potential in blurring and obfuscating the lines of legibility and practicality, pushing the boundaries of emotional expressiveness and allowing for unusual approaches in modern graphic design. "New Aesthetic" considers type design as an opportunity to create art: looking at type design with a benevolence to experiments and processes, and finding potential in the unusual, that might point us into a new future of practicing visual communication.

The Editors

Acide
Laura Csocsán

Acide is a serif font that was designed as an attempt to exaggerate the characteristics serif elements have in a non-traditional way. Serifs are prolonged and their directions are diverted, resulting almost in collisions and extreme situations within and between characters. Rounded and angular letters have less balance than usual, which provide words with a rhythmic and characteristic look when rounded and angular forms follow each other. It started as a lettering work —which was rejected later on—but served as the starting point for the full character set. Acide works best in display situations and short texts. It has a strong presence and its spikes make it a rather hostile face resembling unreadable carvings.

Classification
Serif

Styles
Regular Slanted

Release
N/A

Contact
lauracsocsan.com
lauracsocsan.xyz
@cs__laura

Character overview on page 206

FUTURE IS

NOSTALGIC

ACUDE

Airaz
Javier Unknos

Airaz was initially conceptualized and designed during the Escola Lateral 2019 course as a reflection of normality from a subjective point of view, resulting in typography with its own personality and unique construction maintaining cohesion between the characters. The typography is built with three modules adapted at will to fit and result in forms with certain readability. This personal and random character is reflected in the name "Airaz", which is a local word from my grandfather's village located in Navarra (Spain) which means "sudden gust of strong wind".

Classification
Non-Pixel Semi-Mono Display

Styles
Regular

Release
2020

Contact
javierunknos.com
@javierunknos

ATRAZ

FAMILY NAME
ATRAZ

UNICODE RANGES
BASIC LATIN
LATIN-1 SUPPLEMENT
LATIN EXTENDED-A

DESIGNER
JAVIER UNKNOS

CLASSIFICATION
NON-PIXEL
SEMI-MONO
DISPLAY

DESIGNER URL
HTTPS://JAVIERUNKNOS.COM

STYLES
REGULAR

DESIGNER IG
@JAVIERUNKNOS

AXES COORDINATES
WEIGHT: 500

COPYRIGHT
COPYRIGHT © 2020
BY JAVIER UNKNOS.
ALL RIGHTS RESERVED.

GLYPHS
№:313

RELESE DATE
JANUARY 2020

METRICS
ASCENDER: 700
CAP HEIGHT: 700
X-HEIGHT: 700
DESCENDENT: 0
ITALIC ANGLE: 0º

POSTER SIZE
169.7MM×240MM+5MM BLEED

COLORS
C=0% M=0% Y=0% K=100%

STATUS
AVAILABLE

Aldiviva
Victor Gérard

Aldiviva is a modern interpretation of 'Vivaldi' typeface, originally designed by Peter Friedrich in 1994. Aldiviva was born in 2019 in La Cambre (BE), originally in a single weight which tries to keep the very calligraphic side of the Vivaldi, but using no bezier curves. It was only after the calligraphic weight had been designed that a line version (ultralight), a light version where you can feel the influence of the original ductus, as well as an ultrabold version (really display) were designed. Aldiviva thus became a family of 4 Styles, a display typeface (perhaps more than the original Vivaldi typeface) which remains surprisingly legible in small size for the Primavera & Estate Styles.

Classification
Calligraphic

Styles
Primavera
Estate
Autunno
Inverno

Release
2019

Contact
@gerardpointfr

Character overview on page 208

Alna
Alff Rosine

Alna is an All Caps Display typeface born with a daily calligraphic sketch exploration focused on recurrent diagonal stroke and reverse contrast inspired by Bastarda and 16th century French Caractères de Civilité forebears St Augustine Civilité. The customised retail typeface offers a stable but full of life feeling. Equiped with a bag full of alternates and ligatures for reading optimisation, Alna owns whimsical personality and rhythmic shines at large sizes.

Classification
Display

Styles
Regular

Release
2020

Contact
alffrosine.com
@alff.rosine

FLOWED DISPLAY TYPEFACE

DESIGNED BY WOLDEN BORGOTTON

HAND STYLE-MEGO, OK

HOW KOSHEL, MCMXX

Ampersand
Fatih Hardal

Ampersand reflects the past and future together. It has been inspired by the works of art and design coming from past to present and aims for an aesthetic and modern look. The typeface acts as a link between art and contemporary influences and trends. The 2019 version contains 2 types of characters (both majuscule only). The OpenType format is available for Macintosh and Windows.

Classification
Serif

Styles
Regular
Bold

Release
2019

Contact
hardalstudio.com
@_hardal

Character overview on page 210

ALBEN LAURA LEE

BERMAN FELIX

CAFLISCH MAX

FRIEDMAN DAN

GERSTNER KARL

GÜRTLER ANDRE

KAO GRACE

LUIDL PHILIPP

ODERMATT SIEGFRIED

SCHMID HELMUT

Angels Racing
Mārcis Lapiņš

Angels Racing's beginnings were drawn from the research on street racing whilst looking at aftermarket tuning brand identities. The initial design process started with speedy calligraphy attempts that eventually evolved into a selection of more distinct shapes. This research of shapes, angles, distances, and radiuses worked as a base for a modular system to construct Angels Racing typeface later on.

Classification
Decorative

Styles
Regular

Release
2019

Contact
lapinsmarcis@gmail.com
@marcis.lapins

Character overview on page 211

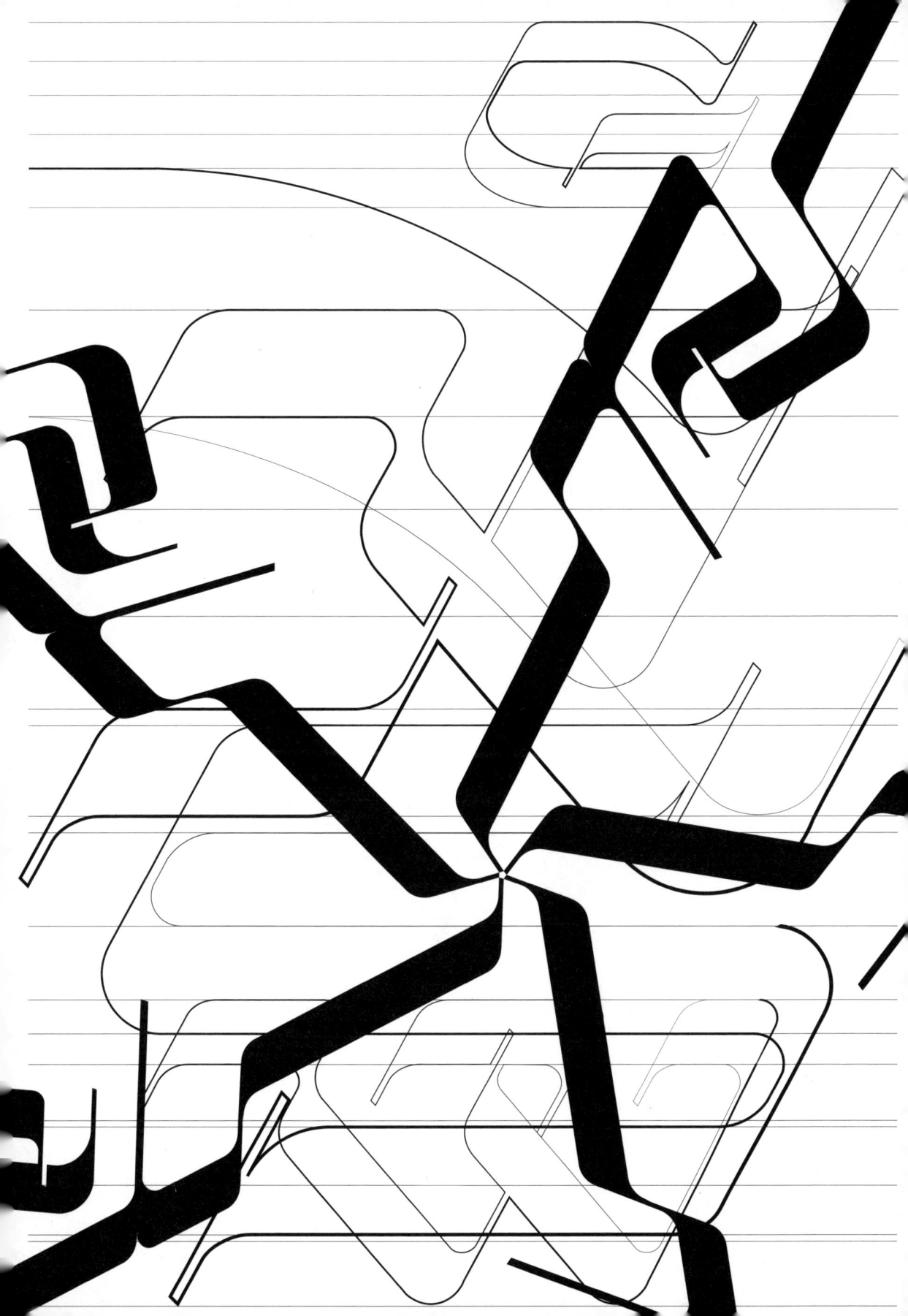

Ara
Felix Sandvoß

ARA basically developed out of my my interest in Arabic culture. It became an experimental Display Typeface inspired by the cover of the Italian downtempo CD "Vajra" compiled in 2006 by DJ Josko (Giorgio Gatti). Artwork credits are going to Simone Mecozzi (member of Gaiatech Project). With its mesmerizing arabesque ornaments it feels fre$h beneath recent underground genres such as Tribal, Downtempo and Ambient. While catching the contemporary spirit of the age in a more ironic way, it can complete edgy/trashy 2000er-L0v€ graphics as well (e.g. the poster artwork to your right).

Classification
Experimental Oriental

Styles
Regular

Release
2020

Contact
felix.sandvoss@gmx.com
@felix_sandvoss

Character overview on page 212

Archimède
3,Quatorze

Originally thought for the visual identity of 3,Quatorze, the Archimède typeface is a Roman serif. The strength and character of this type was inspired by the evolution of the Greek (-750 BP) to the Roman (1 CR) alphabet. The uppercases and lowercases were built with the same grid and their similar sizes and multiple ligatures allow an impressive stylistic game. The Archimède typeface is a characteristic type intended for headings. It has 171 ligatures, 48 Greek signs, 163 Romanesque signs, 29 punctuations and 42 symbols.

Classification
Serif

Styles
Regular

Release
2019

Contact
contact@3-quatorze.fr
3-quatorze.fr
@3-quatorze

ARP3
Ciarán Brandin

Design in response to music is not a revolutionary concept. For years designers have been creating album covers, flyers, posters, and fonts to compliment a band's style and sound. In late 2019, I found myself enjoying the album Shadows (from UK producer Floating Points) and thinking, "Wow, wouldn't it be fun to make a typeface that visualizes the organic, flowing nature of the bass-line in juxtaposition to the mechanical overlay of synths?" As such, ARP3 was born. Forged from strong geometric shapes connected by soft exaggerated curves, ARP3's static styles captures the essence of its title song, while the variable component modulates the letterforms as if reacting to the composition of the music itself.

Classification
Display

Styles
Thin, Thin Italic
Extra Light, Extra Light Italic
Light, Light Italic
Normal, Normal Italic
Regular, Regular Italic
Medium, Medium Italic
Bold, Bold Italic
Ultra Bold, Ultra Bold Italic
Heavy, Heavy Italic

Release
2020

Contact
ciaranbrandin.com
@ciaranbrandin

Character overview on page 214

Arthemys
Morgane VanTorre

Arthemys is a meticulous and generous serif typeface, designed by the Paris based graphic & type designer Morgane VanTorre. Based on XVIIIth century aesthetic, it is born to the meeting of a Nicolas Gando's specimen and engraved letters of cartographies. Thought for display, this typeface underlines a singular union between shapes from the past and a contemporary eye: a kind of fruitful revival which highlights the sensitivities of two eras. The graphic particularities (especially the ligatures set) of Arthemys enable any text to get both a delicate and majestic value.

Classification
Serif

Styles
Light
Regular
Medium
DemiBold
Bold
ExtraBold
Bitmap

Release
2020

Contact
morgane.vantorre@hotmail.fr
morganevantorre.com
@gagane

Character overview on page 215

SERIF KILLER SQUAD

ARTHEMYS

DISPLAY

Serif typeface
amily designed by
© Morgane   Van Torre † 2020

Autark
Stefanie Vogl

Autark is a font based on the feeling of being autonomous, self-sufficient and independent. There-fore, the essence of the typeface is self-confident, dynamic and has a handwritten character. A confident swing, which can be found in the letters b and d, was the starting point for a process in which various components that embody the feeling of being self-sufficient were created. The individual elements gradually turned into letters that finally put a whole alphabet together. Autark can be used stand alone, but also in combination with other fonts, e.g. with Sans.

Classification
Display

Styles
Regular

Release
2020

Contact
@omfdofficial

Character overview on page 216

never ever ever ever believe is false news

B—Sides
Fabio Furlani

This was the custom display typeface for the B—Sides Festival 2020, which takes place in Lucerne, Switzerland. It should look modern and have a summer vibe in it. While designing the typeface, I started to merge the funky serifs together so the font became even more fluid. The ligatures with up to four letters in a row then allowed me to set a tight spacing. All these settings were specifically picked for the information text or artist names. The project was done under the creative direction of Alan Romano and Jaron Gyger who used the typeface to design the poster, website and more.

Classification
Display

Styles
Summer

Release
2020

Contact
fabiofurlani.com
@fabio_furlani_

Character overview on page 217

B-SIDES FESTIVAL 2020
18.-20. JUNI
LUZERN
SONNENBERG
KRIENS

ANGEL BAT DAWID · TINARIWEN
KOKOKO! · BITTER MOON
BISIDES IN CLOUDS · BLIND BUTCHER
CHOCOLATE REMIX · U.V.M.

BRCKHRDT
Gianluca Ciancaglini

The BRCKHRDT typeface was born from the vision of the city and its signs. The forms of the typeface are inspired by social reality, observing its inhabitants and the voices they express through drawings, tags, sprays. The hectic life of the city turns into rhythm, the signs of China Town become lightning bolts, the DNA of the letters. The tags of the young writers are transformed into the curves that define the structure of the alphabet. The typeface wants to communicate the voice of people, expressed through architecture and urban planning.

Classification
Display

Styles
Regular

Release
2020

Contact
@ciancaglinigianluca

Character overview on page 218

BS Malus
Mads-Emil Luplau, Bayonet Services

My friend describes BS Malus as "slab serif masquerading as a fraktur" and while this statement is somewhat problematic—because BS Malus really has no reference to fraktur typefaces—there is a grain of truth behind the description. BS Malus' unique feature is the ink traps when the stems meet the counters, which is made with a reminiscence of the broad nib pen. This feature makes the glyphs more dynamic and gives them some similarities to fraktur typefaces. The brackets at the ascender are slightly angled and dots over the i's have a reference to the calligraphic alphabet. It is a font that works best for display purposes. It will eventually be available in bold and italic as well.

Classification
Slab Serif

Styles
Regular

Release
2020

Contact
@bayonet.services

slab
serif

MAS
QUE
RAD
ING

BS MALUS
SECOND EDITION
2020

DESIGNED BY
BAYONET SERVICES
COPENHAGEN

as
fraktur

My friend described
BS Malus as "a slab serif
masquarading as fraktur"

Chili
Daniel Hermes

Chili typeface started as an experimental project. The whole font is basically built on two clean forms. A square and a rectangle, both with rounded corners. By placing the forms together and overlaying them, letters started to form themselves out of it. Then more and more letters of the alphabet started growing. Suddenly, a typeface was born—which in parts looked like the shape of chili peppers. Next, I started to design the different letters more and more out of its topic and inspiration of the form of a chili pepper. Out of that experimental process arises Chili typeface, which can be used as a display font. Through its soft and sharp forms the typeface gets pointy and very loud, maybe even hot.

Classification
Experimental Display

Styles
Regular

Release
2020

Contact
@_danielhermes_

FEATURED IN:
NEW AESTHETIC VOL.2

CHILI
"TYPEFACE"

AVAILABLE
IN 2020

CHILI
TYPE
FACE

POINT AND
GEOMETRIC

BASED ON TWO
CLEAN FONTS

WITH ROUND AND
EDGT PARTS

TO BE RELEASED IN:

2020:

IS A EXPERIMENTAL
DISPLAY FONT——

DESIGNED BT DANIEL HERNES

© 2020
————— REGULAR CUT

INSPIRED BT
CHILI PEPPERS

IT COMBINES
SHARP ELEMENTS

WITH SOFT LINES
AND FORMS

Conztel
Baptiste Bernazeau

Conztel is a rounded black letter typeface. Structurally, it draws its origins in uncial and cal-ligraphic models, while the envelope is based entirely on vertical and horizontal stems, and thin left-to-right ascending diagonals. It's a really rudimentary system, almost modular, but the variety of letter skeletons provides rich possibilities throughout the alphabet, and for additional decorative glyphs. Aesthetically, the goal was to produce a light hearted iteration of the big black letters family, with rounded stems, rounded intern corners, and open counter forms. The type-face is also influenced by the constellation figures, consisting of basic groupings of connected stars. Overall, the system obviously allows a good number of new iterations to be explored in the future. Who knows?

Classification
Cute Black Letter

Styles
Regular

Release
2020

Contact
forge.cestainsi.online
@baptiste.bernazeau
@cestainsi.funfactory

Character overview on page 221

AreWeAlone?

ZodiacHotLines
CosmicLove

ABCDEFGHIJKLMN
OPQRSTUVWXYZ
abcdefghijklmn
opqrstuvwxyz
0123456789

OpenEyes
InfiniteNight

StarsAlign
SolarFlares
PoeticEights
SunTirade
MoonParade
AstroBallade

FamilyTime
VoûteCéleste
CONZIEL

Dalmata
Stefan Mader

Dalmata is a display typeface that is named after the southern part of Croatia—Dalmatia. The formal language of the typeface establishes a reference to the brutalist-looking war memorials (Spomeniks), which appear in large numbers in this region. The architecture usually appears strange, deterrent, but also playful, fragile and sensitive. Dalmata picks up this contrast and makes use of these different stylistic elements and thereby acquires its very own, comical, but also cheerful character. This aesthetic is a kind of contemporary witness to the often dark past, but with a focus on the positive and new.

Classification
Display

Styles
Bold

Release
2020

Contact
@stefan.mader

Character overview on page 222

Dedale
Awista Montagne

Dedale, or Daedalus, was an inventor, architect and sculptor in Greek mythology. He created the labyrinth, an elaborate and confusing structure, for King Minos of Crete to hold the Minotaur at Knossos. Dedale Display is an experimental typeface, inspired by the representations of the labyrinth on the old silver coins from Knossos (400 BC). I decided to mirror the maze component of the myth in my typeface. I purposefully focused on the complexity of this typeface, making it confusing and difficult to comprehend at first sight. Taking one's time and concentration are key to both solving the maze and deciphering this typeface. Thanks to the small leading, some letters overlap and create an intriguing pattern. The work is still in progress.

Classification
Display

Styles
Regular

Release
2020

Contact
behance.net/Awista
@awista_3YK

Character overview on page 223

DG Sinusoide
Davide Melotti

Letters are for sure the most powerful symbols humans have created. They are sounds translated in symbols with the purpose of communicating. Brilliant! DG Sinusoide was born from this very concept, the visualization of sound. One of the most popular ways to visualise a sound is a sinusoid curve. I drew a lot of sinusoids, cut them in pieces, adapted their sizes and orientation and then composed each glyph with those curves. The final touch was to link each letter to the other letters around them—like each sound links to another—to compose a word in the spoken language. I have to thank the 365typefaces community for suggesting me to work on the concept of sound.

Classification
Display

Styles
Regular

Release
2019

Contact
@dubbio_gusto

Character overview on page 224

dubbiogusto

Eclect
Gregory Page

Eclect is the result of months of type-testing and experimentation that have been documented and showcased on Instagram almost every weekend for over a year. Most of these type try-outs began with basic geometric shapes and evolved into more complex and conceptual forms. Additionally, each experiment led to the next. I wanted the outcome to be bold in terms of thickness but also to include extreme contrasts and angles in some of the letters—a mix between thick and thin; curved and straight. A process of rotating, inverting, distorting caused some of the characters' drawings to be experimental as stand-alone letters; legibility was pushed to the limits. But this is the result I was expecting and what gives its personality. Eclect's joyful overall look and feel will also let you build your own abstract visuals by combining one, two, three or more of these characters together. Let's play!

Classification
Display

Styles
Regular

Release
2020

Contact
@gregory_page_

Character overview on page 225

191 PORTOBELLO
ROAD   ELECTRIC
CINEMA
CO.UK

ELECTRIC

NOTTING
HILL

CINEMA
CINEMA

LONDON

Eryn
Pauline Sesniac

Eryn is inspired by Art Nouveau style. It is based on the aesthetic of flowing lines and the presence of asymmetric rhythms, exemplarily exploited by the artists that took part in the Jugendstil movement, claiming a resurgence of nature and mythology in the arts. Through its promotion of a formal language, the letter becomes image and perpetuates William Blake's illuminated poems. The letter refers to the imaged environment the same way the furniture refers to the natural one: Eryn dwells its own image decorum by creating a slightly fantastic narrative. It is technically conceived from Roman characters and has then emancipated thanks to its graceful arabesques.

Classification
Flourishing Display

Styles
Eryn Nouveau

Release
2020

Contact
paulinesesniac.com
@pauline.ssnc

Character overview on page 226

ERYN NOUVEAU

ABCDEFGHIJKLMNOPQRSTUVWXYZ

PIPING DOWN THE VALLEY WILD
PIPING SONGS & PLEASANT GLEE
ON A CLOUD I SAW A CHILD
AND HE LAUGHING SAID TO ME
PIPE A SIT THERE DOWN AND WRITE
I A BOOK THAT ALL MAY READ

INTRODUCTION TO THE
SONG OF INNOCENCE
BY WILLIAM BLAKE

Eyck
Péter Polacsek

Eyck is a serif typeface with roots in the mythology of the lowland countries. The process started by making a serif without any specific intention or direction in early 2020. This was fine in terms of learning, but I wanted it to be more expressive. I've gradually developed the concept that's surrounding it along with its personality. It's organic shapes derive from the idea of sacred trees which was a popular belief in the Netherlands in the early Middle-Ages. Eyck represents a fusion of Roman and Gothic styles, while it also bears a passive-aggressive personality where the sequence of letterforms results in continuous tension and release.

Classification
Serif

Styles
Regular

Release
2020

Contact
peterpolacsek.com
@noelle.io

Character overview on page 227

Granite Tours

Tia nt cores evel etur ev siatiae
pel iur am optat escep Quias sa
d ne si ra in nus quaec atqui re cones ut
aci dolescipsam ips volores am alibus
s dolut ut molupta t aut dio comni quint
to magnimi utaqutu oria sum aut hicil eum
od ut esercil labore ut em quam sunt ut id
illatus et escepudit aut t aut fugia dolum quint
ant ullabor eriaesed que magnitis pa nimolores

Qu ntum   Particle

United Company

U sites inulparis ali quibus volor sin obis etus
cea nis mod molu mpossi beaturit cis asped
quunt venimagnis st officti onsec bus et
omnimas imolect ur quibus dis et s ium eum sit
ipicili geniatum a eosandem Na aspero et of
tecto que eveni at imus aut od dundae sun
hicabore to de tatur alita aut t am lam vo ptaest
occaborpore y um fugiam ei ota volore se audam
ut landandan atuscias et

Adit venihil labor ciis seque
auta dem ditat qu venimilis
eum quidentur

Enchantm t

Quantum   Pa tic

Base

Rem repro c lenih icius
Ciumquatur Sa ed quaerum iatisimus
nulparcia nesedicten rcipis a llam iusan
imagnis repuda illuptas um t prat re
diame omnihil in c rupe ea volupta
sperferuptat har qui d em quunt
es magnatas milli se de Dia vore ti omnia
ut pro que ellatur a que labore con corupta
quidend ucitiorumque t inus

Zero

Feeeels Fuzzy
Jack Halten Fahnestock

Feeeels Fuzzy, the typeface, is the result of a low-budget commission for the first issue—the "fuzzy" issue—of a magazine called Feeeels. I began the design process by defining its overarching theme; included were interpretations of fuzziness as a state of mind, a type of logic, and a way of rendering or resolution. I thought the idea of "low resolution" had a lot of potential in terms of form-making so I focused on that area. I did some sketching—both on paper and screen—using various pixelation and halftone techniques until I found something interesting that I was happy with. The typeface follows two core design decisions. The first involves mixing letterforms of standard contrast—thicker vertical than horizontal strokes—with those of reverse contrast—thinner vertical than horizontal strokes. This juxtaposition yields a very unusual typographic rhythm. The second involves widening letterforms asymmetrically and randomly—perhaps with a "fuzzy" logic.

Classification
Multi-Contrast Grotesque

Styles
Regular

Release
2019

Contact
jackf.me
@jckfa

Character overview on page 228

FF Duerer
Fabian Franz

Sometimes it can be done in no time. A few timely shapes that repeat, a few strange curves, a little bit of interpretation and you have 26 glyphs. 26 glyphs that are far from perfect—but what is really perfect in 2020? To be honest: Very few fonts survive for decades. And FF Duerer does not even plan to outlast a complete project. For this reason, everyone gets it for free. Maybe for a poster, a last minute voucher for the parents-in-law or as a template for your own projects. Take it, divide it, cut it, kern it, clean it. You decide what the typeface deserves and what happens to it.

Classification
Custom

Styles
Light

Release
2020

Contact
fabianfranz.com
@f.ffffranz

Character overview on page 229

TWENTYBIX
GLYPHS
MAKE NO
TYPEFACE
BUT A
FUNDAMENT
SERVICES
POSTER

SSBY9DBM
ALL SYSTEM
KIND DETAIL
LIGHT AND
AT PROCESS

TWENTYLINDBAL

Fluse
Victor Pesotsky

Fluse was designed on a simple formalistic idea: Switching from a thick vertical stroke to a narrow horizontal stroke. Transients ensure that the shape is rounded and flows into another. These fillets are also passed into the construction of graphemes. Fluse is an accidental sans-serif font. The font is suitable for both active titles and medium-sized texts. It can also be an accent in a poster or the basis of a corporate identity. Fluse font supports Basic Latin, Cyrillic and certain other languages. The font has one Regular style.

Classification
Decorative

Styles
Regular

Release
2020

Contact
behance.net/viiktoor
@vviiktoor

Character overview on page 230

FLUSE

Despite being a constructed language

Fluse font supports Basic Latin, Cyrillic and certain other languages.
The font has one Regular weight.

translation

L H R

Forsaken
Nicolas Terzian

The very concept of this typeface was to choose a place or a building, to study its historical, architectural, social aspects, and make it a typeface. This concept was introduced to me by my teacher and graphic designer Maroussia Jannelle in her course. The place I chose is "Le Palacio d'Abraxas" in Noisy-le-Grand, my hometown near Paris. This place always fascinated me by its architectural aspect. It looks like an old Greek Palace in a suburban environment. But by studying its social and historical aspects, a shocking truth came to me: This place was forsaken by the city and its architect, the famous and infamous Ricardo Bofill. With all this in mind, I decided to focus on symmetry, experimental serif, and a system that would make the characters downfalling, a typeface representing "Le Palacio", that would forsake its purpose.

Classification
Modular Serif

Styles
Display
Display Sans

Release
2020

Contact
nizegraphiks@gmail.com
@nztrz_

Character overview on page 231

Gallique
Emma Marichal

I first thought of the project as a variable typeface. I began with a raw and fat version in order to carve out a very thin font, "like a shiny diamond". I then pushed the design further, concluding that it makes her "think of a rose: elegant but dangerous and sharped". Gallique takes its name from a rose: Rosa gallica. This duality between the petals' softness and the prickle of the thorn led the design of its forms. For ligatures lovers, Gallique is made to tangle, intertwine itself and display its delicate and hypnotic curves. Elegant by its vegetal shapes but aggressive by its serifs, Gallique is a display which has currently one style: Light.

Classification
Display-Serifs

Styles
Light

Release
2020

Contact
emmamarichal.fr
@emmarichal

Character overview on page 232

GANG
Floriane Rousselot

GANG typeface is a mix of different inspirations from letters found mostly in NY streets to hand-written shapes. I first worked on some handwritten letters with the idea of using a minimum of movement/lines. GANG has been designed with more finesse and thin contrasts, bringing in the idea of calligraphic aspect. So GANG is the meeting of grafitti from Brooklyn with calligraphic style, and different shapes, like shapes from Hebrew letters on some buildings, graffiti, street art, car brands, crew signatures, shop signs in different languages. As a result, GANG is a visual concentrate of cultures. Also, I wanted to push forward the boundaries of legibility on each letter, and find a balance to keep the same visual code in order to create a correlation between all the letters.

Classification
Experimental

Styles
Regular

Release
2020

Contact
florianerousselot.com
@floriane.rousselot

Character overview on page 233

ABCDEFGHIJ

KLMNOPQRS

GANG

TUVWXYZ

0123456789

GlyphWorld
Leah Maldonado

GlyphWorld is my contribution to the expressionist type design movement. It's a free typeface of nine fonts. It's set in a mythical alternate font world made of nine landscapes: Forest, Meadow, Flower, Mountain, Airland, Animal Soul, Glacier, Desert, and Wasteland. The project pushes the boundaries of what a typeface can be by using the medium of letterforms to reflect an emotional connection to our environment.

Classification
Script

Styles
Forest
Meadow
Flower
Mountain
Airland
Animal Soul
Glacier
Desert
Wasteland

Release
2019

Contact
leahmaldonado.com
@fun.weirdo

Character overview on page 234

ABCD

EFG

MIJK

LMN

OPQ

RST

UVW

XYZ

Grief
Alexandre Bassi

Grief is a contemporary interpretation of medieval uncial manuscripts and questions the relationship between writing and its translation by digital tools. This typeface attempts to digitally reflect calligraphic features such as the gesture and speed of the hand or the variation in pressure and angle of the nib. Hand-drawing was a crucial phase in the process of creating these types, giving them highly expressive shapes with fine calligraphic details while remaining undeniably contemporary. Based on the scripts of this period, it is entirely composed of uppercase and has a wide variety of alternates which makes this typeface very effective in display.

Classification
Display

Styles
Regular

Release
2020

Contact
alexandrebassi.com
@alexandre___bassi

Character overview on page 235

¶ GRIEF CLOUDS THE INK. A SCRIBE LAMENTS THROUGH HIS QUILL

Hanol
Bouk RA

Hanol emphasizes the beauty of curves on the strands of letters. When I designed this typeface, I was interested in the interaction between the angular shape and the smooth curve. Looking at the first sketch, I imagined tangled hair thanks to the curves that randomly appear in the letters. I focused on this idea and worked on the ligatures and empty spaces between the serif and the curved terminals in sequences of letters to maximize this flexibility in the typeface. While constantly modifying the glyphs, I thought of the celestial robe of a fairy floating in the air in a traditional oriental fairy tale. Inspired by this, I improved the typeface so that it has a light and lively atmosphere.

Classification
Old Style

Styles
Light

Release
2020

Contact
@_bouk_ra_

Character overview on page 236

ABCDEFGHIJKLM
NOPQRSTUVWX

THE TYPEFACE HANOL, INSPIRED BY THE CELESTIAL ROBE OF A FAIRY FLOATING IN THE
IN AN ORIENTAL TRADITIONAL FAIRY TALE, HAS A LIGHT AND LIVELY ATMOSPHERE

Hanol

HfMDK
Massimiliano Audretsch

Together with the Frankfurt University of Music and Performing Arts, we challenged classical corporate design thinking. We deliberately refrained from using a static logo. Instead, we placed the brand on a broad and grounded foundation by developing a complete font family. This is how the HfMDK sets its mark word for word. Agile, lively and in tune with the rhythm of the university. In the HfMDK headline cut, every letter is available in three variations—with increasing "rythm". For writing the new HfMDK logo alone—the word mark with its five characters—there are $3^5 = 243$ possibilities. This means that anyone who uses the font can choose their own variant while typing the text—the unmistakable character of the HfMDK headline ensures its recognisability.

Classification
Grotesk

Styles
Headline Voll
Headline Unten
Headline Oben
Light
Regular
Bold

Release
2019

Contact
gruppo-due.com
gruppo.due
s-t-a-t-e.com

Character overview on page 237

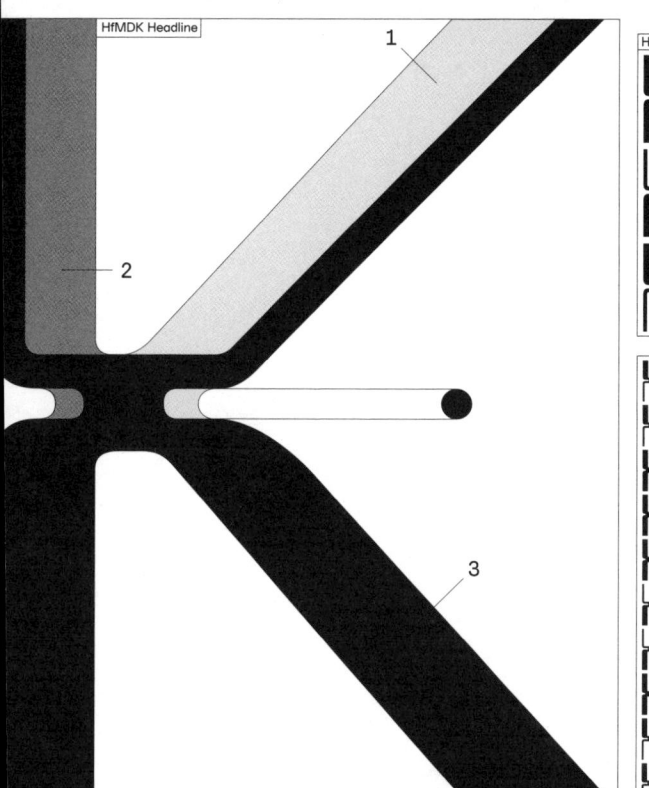

HfMDK Headline

1
2
3

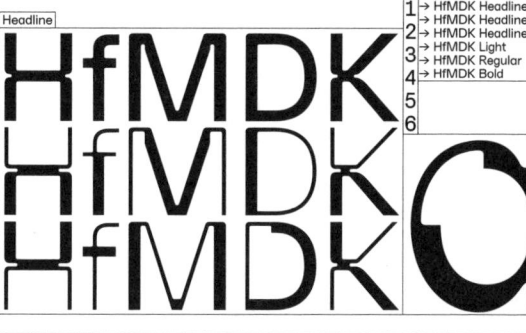

HfMDK
HfMDK
HfMDK

1 →	HfMDK Headline Voll
2 →	HfMDK Headline Unten
3 →	HfMDK Headline Oben
4 →	HfMDK Light
5 →	HfMDK Regular
6 →	HfMDK Bold

a

HfMDK HfMDK HfMDK
HfMDK HfMDK HfMDK
HfMDK HfMDK HfMDK
HfMDK HfMDK HfMDK
HfMDK HfMDK HfMDK
HfMDK HfMDK HfMDK
HfMDK HfMDK HfMDK
HfMDK HfMDK HfMDK
HfMDK HfMDK HfMDK
HfMDK HfMDK HfMDK

✳ ✳ ✳

HfMDK Light + Regular + Bold

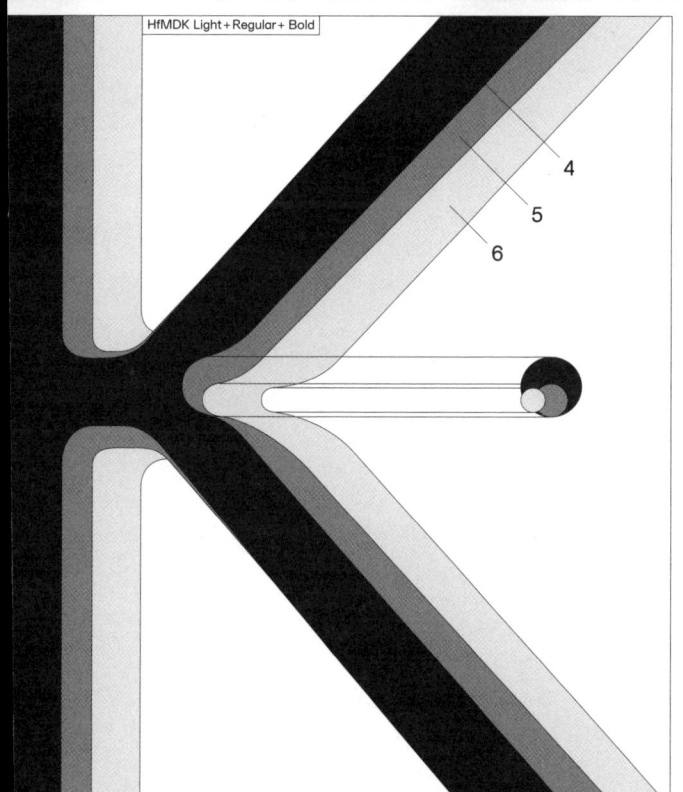

4
5
6

Light + Regular + Bold

HfMDK
HfMDK
HfMDK

ABCDEFGHIJKLMNOPQRSTU
VWXYZÀÁÂÃÄÅĀĄÆÇĆĎ
ĐDEÈÉÊËĒĘĚEGĬÍÎÏİĶLĹĽŁŅŃŇÑ
ŃOÒÓÔÕÖŌŐŒÞRŘSŚŠŞT
TŢUUÙÚÛÜŪŮŰWWWYÝŸ
SŚŽŹŻ

abcdefghijklmnopqrstuvwxyz
aàáâãäåāąæçćďdeèéêëēęěeg
ĭíîïijkĺľłņńňñoòóôõöōőœþŕřŕŕss
ştţuùúûüūůűwwwyýÿßžźż

1234567890

!¡?¿#%/.::...[\{_}(*)›«‹»
+-−×÷∞=∅↑↓↔→←
∅/●●●●●●●● ✶✷✸✴✹✺

ABCDEFGHIJKLMNOPQRST
UVWXYZÀÁÂÃÄÅĀĄÆÇ
ĆĎĐDEÈÉÊËĒĘĚEGĬÍÎÏİĶLĹĽŁ
ŅŃŇÑŃOÒÓÔÕÖŌŐŒÞRŘR
WYÝŸSŚŽŹŻ

abcdefghijklmnopqrstuvwxyz
aàáâãäåāąæçćďdeèéêëēęěe
ĭíîïijkĺľłņńňñoòóôõöōőœþŕř
sştţuùúûüūůűwwwyýÿßžźż

1234567890

!¡?¿#%/.::...[\{_}(*)
+-−×÷∞=∅
∅/●●●●●●●●

ABCDEFGHIJKLMNOPQRS
TUVWXYZÀÁÂÃÄÅĀĄÆ
ÇĆĎĐDEÈÉÊËĒĘĚEGĬÍÎÏİĶLĹĽŁ
ŅŃŇÑŃOÒÓÔÕÖŌŐŒÞ
RŘRSŚŠŞTTŢUUÙÚÛÜŪŮŰWW
WSSYÝŸŽŹŻ

abcdefghijklmnopqrstuvwx
yzàáâãäåāąæçćďdeèéêëē
ęěeĭíîïijkĺľłņńňñoòóôõöōőœ
œþŕřŕŕsştţuùúûüūůűwwww
yýÿßžźż

1234567890

!¡?¿#%/.::...[\{_}(*)!¿&&→
+-−×÷∞=∅↑↓↔
∅/●●●●●●●● ✶✷✸ ✴✹✺✻

aaa

...achen:

...zept → State Agentur für Design, Berlin (www.s-t-a-t-e.com)
→ Massimiliano Audretsch (www.gruppo-due.com)

...taltung → Massimiliano Audretsch (www.gruppo-due.com)

MDK | ↳ 2019 | Italic → 2020

Sprachen:
Afrikaans, Albanisch, Asu, Baskisch, Bemba, Bena, Bosnisch, Dänisch, Deutsch, Diola, Englisch, Estnisch, Färöisch, Filipino, Finnisch,
Französisch, Friaulisch, Galicisch, Ganda, Gusii, Inari-Samisch, Indonesisch, Irisch, Isländisch, Italienisch, Kabuverdianu, Kalenjin,
Katalanisch, Kinyarwanda, Kölsch, Kornisch, Kroatisch, Lettisch, Litauisch, Luhya, Luo, Luxemburgisch, Machame, Madagassisch,
Makhuwa-Meetto, Makonde, Malaiisch, Manx, Morisyen, Niederdeutsch, Niederländisch, Niedersorbisch, Nord-Ndebele, Nordsamisch,
Norwegisch Bokmål, Norwegisch Nynorsk, Nyankole, Obersorbisch, Oromo, Polnisch, Portugiesisch, Rätoromanisch, Rombo, Rukiga,
Rundi, Rwa, Samburu, Sango, Sangu, Schottisches Gälisch, Schwedisch, Schweizerdeutsch, Sena, Shambala, Shona, Slowakisch,
Slowenisch, Soga, Somali, Spanisch, Suaheli, Taita, Teso, Tschechisch, Turkmenisch, Ungarisch, Vunjo, Walisisch, Westfriesisch, Zulu

Hidde Grotesk
Matteo Bettini

Hidde is a neo-grotesk typeface with visible and pronunciated inktraps both on the upper and lower case letters. The history behind typefaces that made their fame through the inktrap feature is really long, starting from the well-known Bell Centennial commissioned to Matthew Carter in 1978 to other great examples of the modern age like Retina by Frere-Jones Type in 2016. Nowadays, inktraps are becoming a proper aesthetic feature beyond their previous print functionality. Examples are clearly visible in recent works such as Whyte Inktrap Release by Dinamo in 2019. They are creating another dimension and embody meanings beyond the linguistical one. Hidde stands for a typeface that uses inktraps to unveil another layer of interpretation.

Classification
Grotesk

Styles
Book
Semibold
Black

Release
N/A

Contact
@600mt

Character overview on page 238

Can you call someone who is not a contact?
Can you see when someone was last on Skype?
How do I see all Skype participants?
How many people can join a zoom meeting?
Why am I the only person in the call?

As far as we know, *humans* like to keep certain distances between themselves or things. Unexpectedly the size of this **invisible bubble** of space is used to communicate. Sometimes they stay alone.

Jugendstil
Robin Guillemin

Jugendstil is a typeface inspired by Art Nouveau architectures. The idea of this typeface was born in Lisbon, but built in Paris. During that period, I was fascinated by the objects of furniture and art nouveau architecture that I could observe in these two cities. Jugendstil is characterized by the presence of curves and ornamentations inspired by trees, flowers, insects, and animals. It aims to introduce sensitivity into everday typographic forms. The *terminaisons* of letters are also very organic and asymmetric.

Classification
Serif

Styles
Display

Release
2019

Contact
@robinguillemin

Character overview on page 239

AUSSTELLUNG
Jugendstilmöbel und Architektur

{‡01_/@R*Gbƒ%$
He#QÆ¶[r£®Mji)Ø
§•!?€·12°;:&Âæ→fi}

rkunft des Ausdrucks

Der Ausdruck *Jugendstil* geht zurück auf die von *Georg rth* Ende 1895 in München gegründete illustrierte Kulturzeitschrift gend und ist zu verstehen als eine Gegenbewegung junger Künstler d Kunsthandwerker zum rückwärtsgewandten Historismus, aber h zur als seelenlos verstandenen *Industrialisierung*. Der Blick

richtet sich auf neue Materialien, wie Beton oder Eisen, und neue Baumethoden. Er ist nur im deutschsprachigen Raum, den *Niederlanden, Ungarn,* den *nordischen Ländern* und in *Lettland* in Gebrauch. Von Jugendstil war erstmals im Jahr 1897 bei der *Sächsisch-Thüringischen Industrie-und Gewerbeausstellung Leipzig 1897* die Rede. Hierfür gestaltete Paul Möbius den außergewöhnlichen

Ausstellungspavillon Nietzschmann-Wommer; der Pavillon wurde beschrieben als vom Hergebrachten stark abweichend mit gewagt humoristisch-phantastischen Motiven, die einen gewissen Schwung entwickeln. Äußerlich kennzeichnende Teile oder Elemente des Jugendstils sind dekorativ geschwungene Linien sowie großflächige florale Ornamente.

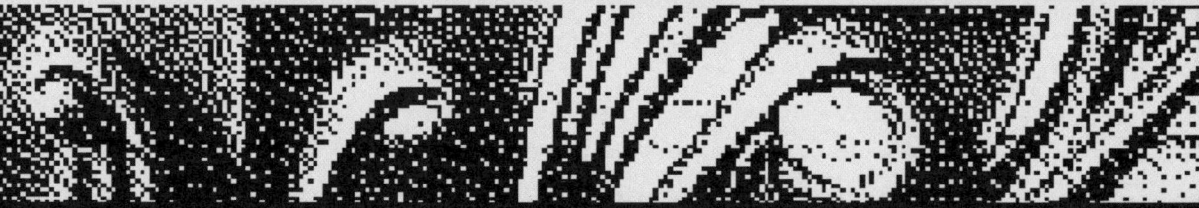

Georg Hirth	Fritz von Uhde	Max Klinger
Peter Behrens	Wilhelm Trübner	August Endel
Hermann Billing	Franz von Stuck	Gustav Klimt
Otto Eckmann	Eugene Spiro	Alfons Mucha

Kasja
Vivien Hoffmann

I'm a fan of letters that communicate something within themselves, besides the words they write. Kasja is one of the first display typefaces I've ever worked on. It was a bit of a flex for me to design a typeface that's barely legible but that looks dangerous and sexy. I found that pretty cool.

Classification
Display

Styles
Regular

Release
2018

Contact
vivienhoffmann.com
@vivien_hoffmann_

Character overview on page 240

eher

then

gern

Hafen

deren

Dort

mitte

Büro

Katsu Grotesque
Daniel Wenzel

Katsu Grotesque is based on the handwriting letterforms of Katsu, a NYC graffiti artist known for his graffiti drones, autonomous graffiti robots, or A.I. art. It originated as a sign of respect and admiration for his work. The starting point was a written "FUCK TRUMP." on a "Memory Foam" exhibition poster, with a very distinguished double-stacked "K" and "R" as well as a "T" and "F" with long arm serifs. After continuously refining the single regular weight over a period of two years, it seemed inevitable to create a monospaced version of the typeface, given that Katsu is a pioneer in combining graffiti and technology. Certain letterforms within his tags, like the lower-case "t" in many "Katsu.BTM." tags, already provided the necessary characteristics.

Classification
Neo-Grotesque

Styles
Light
Regular
Bold
Light Mono
Regular Mono
Bold Mono

Release
2020

Contact
wenzeldaniel.com
@wnzldnl

Character overview on page 241

Grotesq ue Beta

Graffiti

Grotesq

Katsu Grotesq

Handwr

ting

Letters

Kel-Var
Mathias Robert

The creation of Kel-Var began with the desire to represent music graphically, more precisely a song called "Inside the sun" of the band Sleep. The sound was hazy with a lot of reverb but also heavy like a huge storm cloud. The font had to reflect these two aspects. I was inspired by late sixties hippie letterings, but I wanted something more modern and sharper. So it mixes psychedelic curves and bolder straight lines. This contrast creates rhythm and makes the words look abstract.

Classification
Psychedelic

Styles
Display

Release
2019

Contact
@mathias_robert_

Character overview on page 242

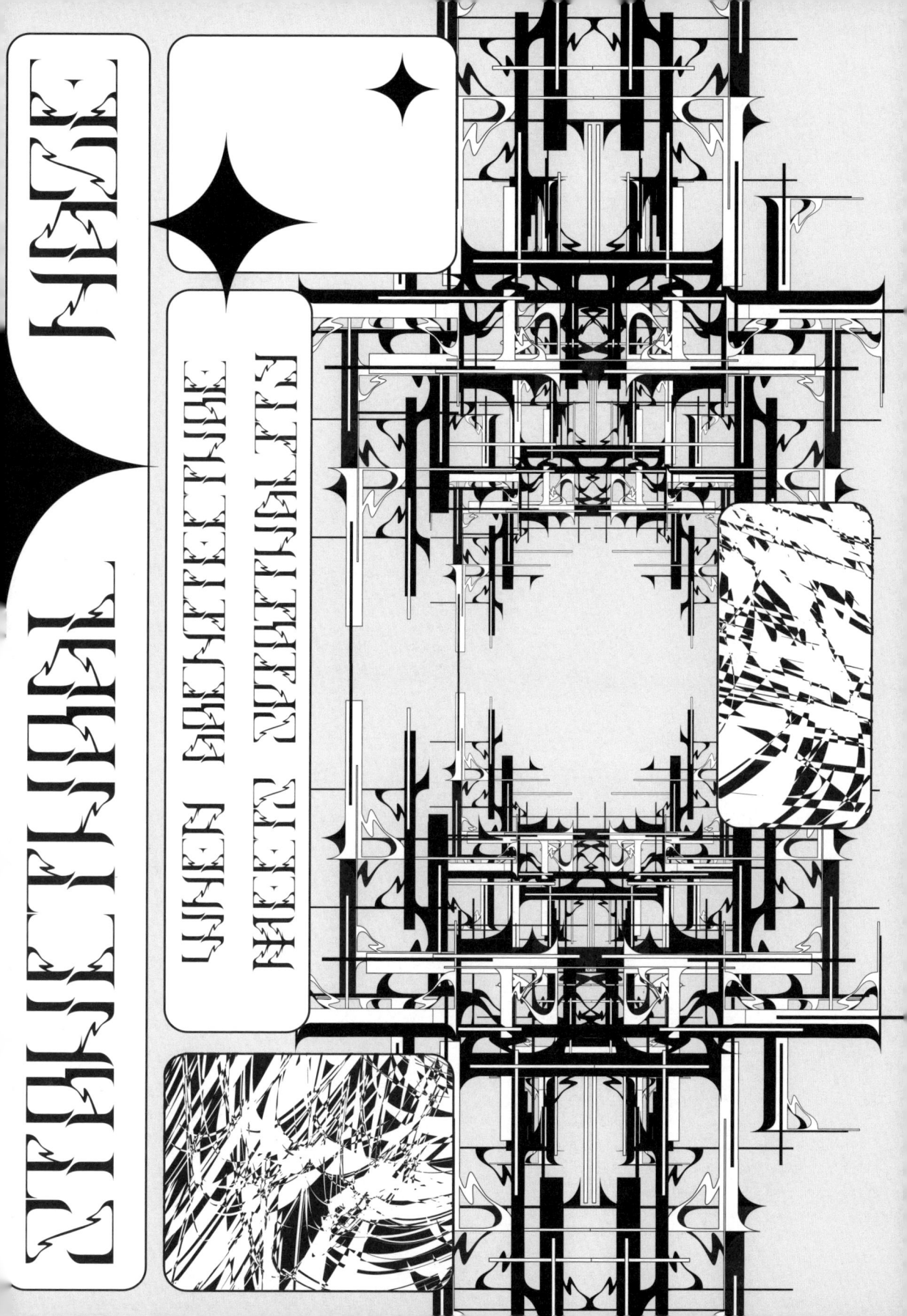

STRUCTURE

HERE

WHEN ARCHITECTURE
MEETS SPIRITUALITY

Kéroïne
Charlotte Rohde

Kéroïne Doux Extrême (2020) is an ultra-soothing daily moisturiser.
It soothes and repairs the skin barrier.
A unique hydrating, re-plumping formula enriched with two pure hyaluronic acids and vitamin B5.
Apply to the face, neck and eye contour once or twice a day.
Smooth, fresh, and melting texture to comfort your skin.
Suitable for allergic or ultra-sensitive skin. Intensely hydrates and soothes skin.
Repairs the skin barrier.
Immediate Hydration: 96%
Long term Hydration: +43% of hydration per T8h.
Rated (10/10)

Classification
Moisturising Serif

Styles
Doux Extrême
Intense Légère
Ultra Riche
Ultra Légère

Release
2020

Contact
charlotterohde.de
@charlotte__rohde

near
far

Aqua
Triethanolamine
Glycerin
Prunus Amygilus
Oil
Paraffinum Liquidum
Hydrolyzed
        Hyaluronic Acid
Tocopheryl Acetate
Cft 42090
        Zinc Sulfate

wherever
you
are™

Keroïne Doux Extrême et Intense Légère, Charlotte Rohde, 2020. Rendering by Hanna Schrage.

Kira
Mickaël Emile

Kira is a tribute to psychopomps who are creatures, spirits, angels, or deities in many religions. Their responsibility is to guide newly deceased souls from Earth to the afterlife. Its name directly refers to the Japanese manga series Death Note, where the main character named Light Yagami is nicknamed "Kira" as a phonetic translation of "killer". Its sharp edges are inspired by both gothic and incised styles, suggesting the timeless and sacred nature of those gods. The stars in some letters can be seen as human souls waiting for their judgement.

Classification
Serif

Styles
Light

Release
2020

Contact
mickaelemile1@gmail.com
mickaelemile.fr
@mickaelemile

Character overview on page 244

Koegi
Zoé Abravanel

Koegi is inspired by several rainbow myths. The iconography of the rainbow can be found in many cultures and religions. It often represents a bridge between heaven and earth. Moreover, in some cultures (Australian Aborigines, Brasilian…) the rainbow can take the form of a celestial snake (Wollunqua, Oxumaré…) As a result, Koegi stems from a mystical and occult universe and its appearance echoes it. As a snake, this font has sinuous curves and sharp edges. Developing Koegi has also involved a lot of experimentations.

Classification
Serif

Styles
Regular

Release
2020

Contact
ostudlez.com
@ostudlez

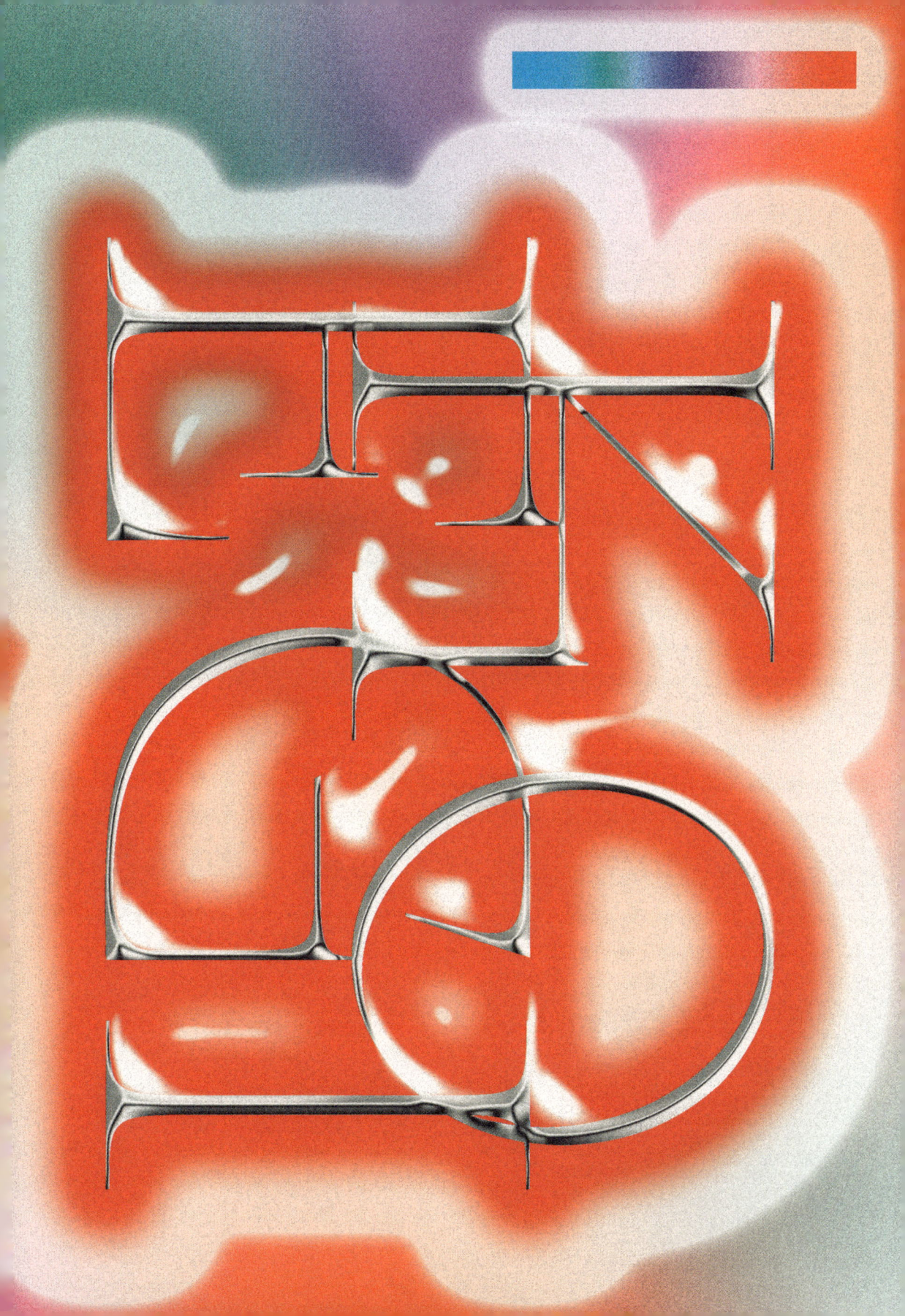

Korosu
Emilie Vizcano

Korosu is a serif typeface of 362 glyphs. Inspired by O-ren Ishii, a fictional character in the movie Kill Bill from Quentin Tarantino (one of my favourites). Korosu means "kill" in Japanese, in reference to O-ren's job: She's a Japanese killer who fights with a saber. I wanted to make a typeface with sharp vibes to wink at the Hattori Hanzo swords of the movie.

Classification
Serif

Styles
Regular

Release
2020

Contact
emilievizcano.com
@emilievizcano

Character overview on page 246

KOROSU

| 40 | 580 | 5 30 | 747 | 30 40 | 622 | 10 30 | 747 | 30 60 | 626 | 60 30 | 689 | 25 |

*362

(Glyphs]

AK

ÆR

ÆB

Qa
Snk.

0%

Korosu – Courant
362 Glyphs

Print & Web licenses

Inspired by O-ren Ishii

Emilie Vizcano
Release : 2020

.otf

DVASQUAÐ

Latin, Western Europe,
Central Europe,
South Eastern Europe

.ttf
.woff
.woff2

ÆKA : Cottonmouth
From : Kill Bill
Quentin Tarantino

Available
upon request

La Bretonnante
Killian Maguet

La Bretonnante is a typography that takes its name from the Celtic and Breton culture in which I have lived since I was a child. Sharpened, it is indeed based on lapidary letters as well as around granite, a material that is mainly found in this region. I particularly wanted to highlight this part of me. This is the result of work done in the manner of a stonemason. These letters are no longer drawn like a type designer, but really cut, mixing several trades into one, which are also found in everyday life.

Classification
Serif

Styles
Granit

Release
2020

Contact
killianmaguet.fr
@diredigglaz

Character overview on page 247

LeBug
Jimmy Auger

LeBug is a titling type that is not going to change the world. :-) I initially started it (in 2018) without really thinking about reworking it one day (in 2020). It was just a training, a hybridization between digital (which smells like a burning fan), and this good old printing press (it stinks of metal, sweat and industrial grease). Pretty basic stuff. While writing this, I realize that I'm really not good at talking about why and how I created this. Anyway, anyway. :-) I hope you'll like these few letters, and this poster, too. Oh, and I forgot: LeBug will be available in its complete and final version in December 2020. And that for free! I just don't know exactly where. Take care of yourself, and don't hesitate to send me a short message lmao! Kiss.

Classification
Display

Styles
Regular

Release
2020

Contact
@jimmypremier

Character overview on page 248

Lily
Antoine Brun

Lily is a display font taking its roots from the Didots found in 19th century books of entomology and plant studies. Following the chimerical theme, Lily is the fusion of different typographic families. In addition, the ligatures, a fusion of two letters (or more), are reinforcing the chimerical aspect. Lily aims to display the typography in a fancy and complex way through her large ligature sets and contrasted lines. At the moment Lily is only available in a fat weight but who knows, a bold version might sprout.

Classification
Serif

Styles
Regular

Release
2020

Contact
@atn_brun

Character overview on page 249

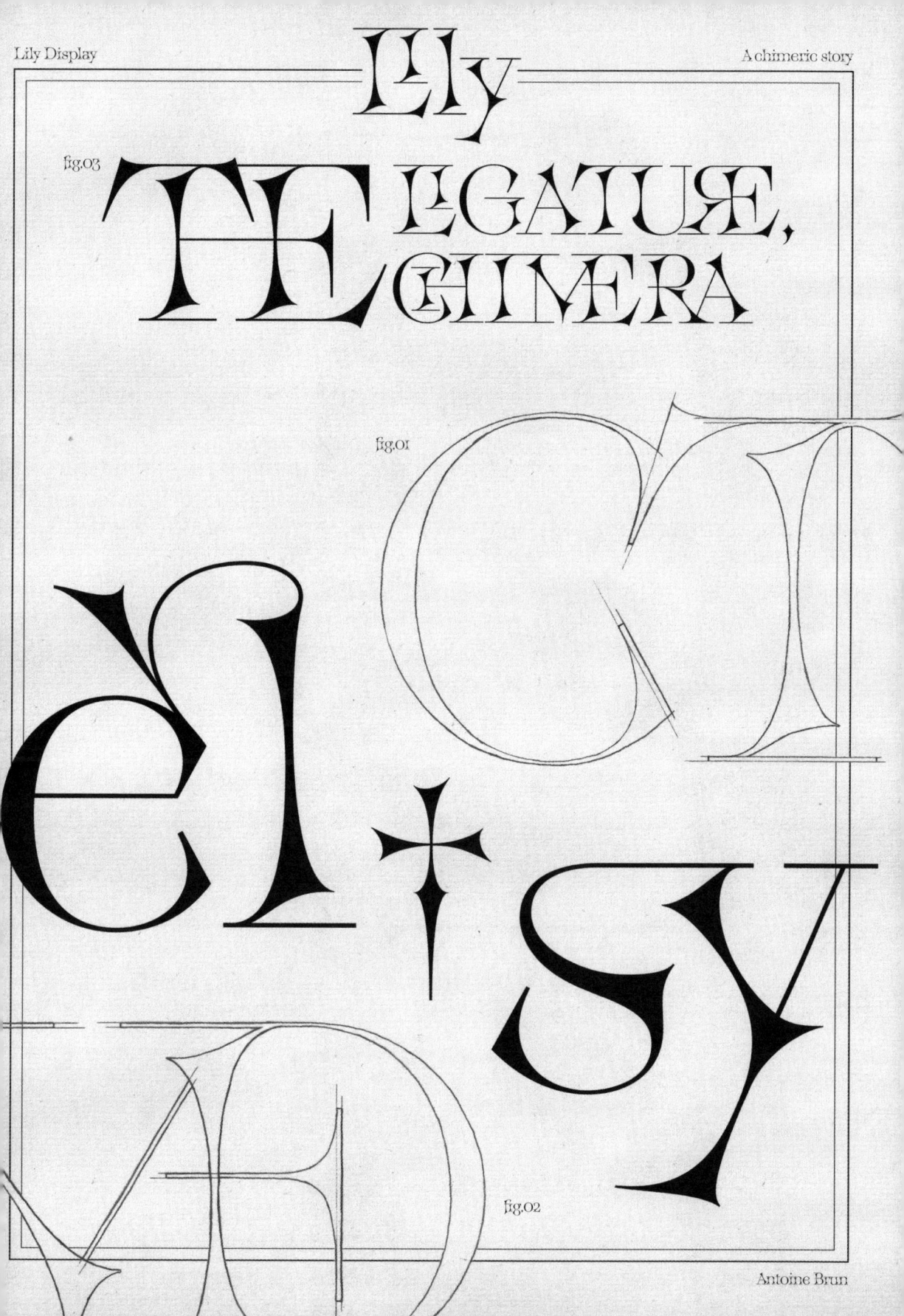

LILY

fig.03

THE LIGATURE, CHIMERA

fig.01

fig.02

Lizard
Robert Gutmann

Lizard was initiated in the hot summer of 2019, when I spent days watching the lively goings-ons of a lizard family in my parents' garden while spending my vacation there. Lizards quickly scamper over rocks, trees and across the ground using their tails to help balance. Usually the encounter with one of those does not last very long. Lizards are quite fast, using locomotion as a primary defense tactic. The hand drawn typeface is inspired by the reptile of the same name. The result is a font that is sensitive, almost fragile but elegant in its movement at the same time, always seeking for a good balance between it. Lizard is supposed to be used as a display typeface and is available on request.

Classification
Decorative

Styles
Regular

Release
2020

Contact
@robert_gutmann

Character overview on page 250

Lobular
Ariel Martín Pérez

Lobular is a typeface that looks like cross-sections of kidneys, or like fine transversal slices of an intestinal tract. It creates black masses on the page's surface, in which light is ensnared when it enters the core of the letters. One of its main features is its entirely flat inktraps (the only straight lines in the typeface), which don't have the practical purpose of avoiding bleeding in print, but rather a structural role for drawing the counters. Its design also recalls that of bubble alphabets, commonly seen in graffiti tags in many places around the world. All in all, designing Lobular was a matter of solving topological problems (keeping curves and gaps consistent). Sometimes this constraint was also used as an inspiration to create experimental letterforms.

Classification
Organic

Styles
Regular

Release
2020

Contact
contact@arielgraphisme.com
arielgraphisme.com
@ariel_martin_perez

Character overview on page 251

TOTALLY VEGAN

AND ROUNDILICIOUS

LOBULAROGENICNESS

RESTAURANTS

GO!!!!!! ALL THE WAY MUM

THE QUICK BROWN
FOX JUMPS OVER
THE LAZY SAUSAGE

LOBULAR
RESEARCH
FACILITIES™

Macchia
Brando Corradini

Macchia type was born from the desire to create well-defined alphabet letters. At the end of the project, it evolved into the typeface used in my poster, in which each individual letter is contained within a square. Certainly this type is particular and unconventional. I wanted it to capture the stain that the street artist leaves when he sprays murals.

Classification
Decorative

Styles
Regular

Release
2019

Contact
brandocorradini.com
@brando.corradini

Character overview on page 252

Magdalene
Leah Maldonado

Magdalene is the embodiment of all of my mean qualities. It speaks in a rude monotone and rolls its eyes at its reader. Magdalene selfishly breaks the rules of a monospace to allow multiple ligatures between characters. Although it has a sour attitude it cannot help but convey a sense of beauty, too. A scream in the right pitch can sound like a song.

Classification
Monospace

Styles
Mono

Release
2020

Contact
leahmaldonado.com
@fun.weirdo

Character overview on page 253

ACCORD TO AN WORD SHOULD BE LINK

i make these letters late at night and early in the morning their shapes begin to hypnotize me i consider the other authors hypnotized just like me i tweet that im tired and should go to bed i tweet that im up late again making letters my twitter followers

i consider these creations little emotions packed into the shape of a letter like a noise is packed into the string of a guitar i author these noises for the sake of others to use over and over will those future users consider me as i consider them i think this quietly to myself

so much time and effort is embedded in an S i painfully construct this letter always early in the morning never looking right never seeming balanced it feels like spinning over and over i spin yet still the S is wrong to my future user i use the S as a love letter

Mars
Rémi Volclair

I started this typo a year ago during a school project where we had to make a poster on Marseille. I started to create shapes that reminded me of the Mistral, which is a common wind in Marseille. After the first edition, I took the drawings to create a second edition which is not made of forms, but is more applied to the curve. The poster is in honor of the city of Marseille. It is playing a tyography game—mixing the Neue Haas Grotesk and the Mars—to generate interesting contrasts. Besides the wind, football has an important place in the city and therefore I decided to put Olympique de Marseille (OM) on the poster.

Classification
Display

Styles
Light

Release
2019

Contact
@rembagram

Character overview on page 254

Monolog
Lennart Van den Bossche

Monolog started as a logo design for a Belgian clothing brand that was selling kimonos. I started playing with shapes resembling draping and folded fabric. Making combinations with these shapes until I could see letters in them, it was becoming way too wicked for the client I was working for. But I was so psyched that I lost complete interest in the client and just continued with the typeface. At that time, I was listening a lot to the "korg funk 5" track of Aphex Twin made on a Korg Monologue. The name Monolog is a reference to that. As all my other typefaces, this one is still in progress. The ultimate goal of Monolog is to have a lot of alternatives. When typing it, the image of words will constantly change as every letter combination will act as a different ligature. This typeface is not about legibility, but about composition and shapes.

Classification
Decorative

Styles
Irregular

Release
2020

Contact
lennartvandenbossche.com
@lennart_van_den_bossche
Ultral3nny.tumblr.com

Character overview on page 255

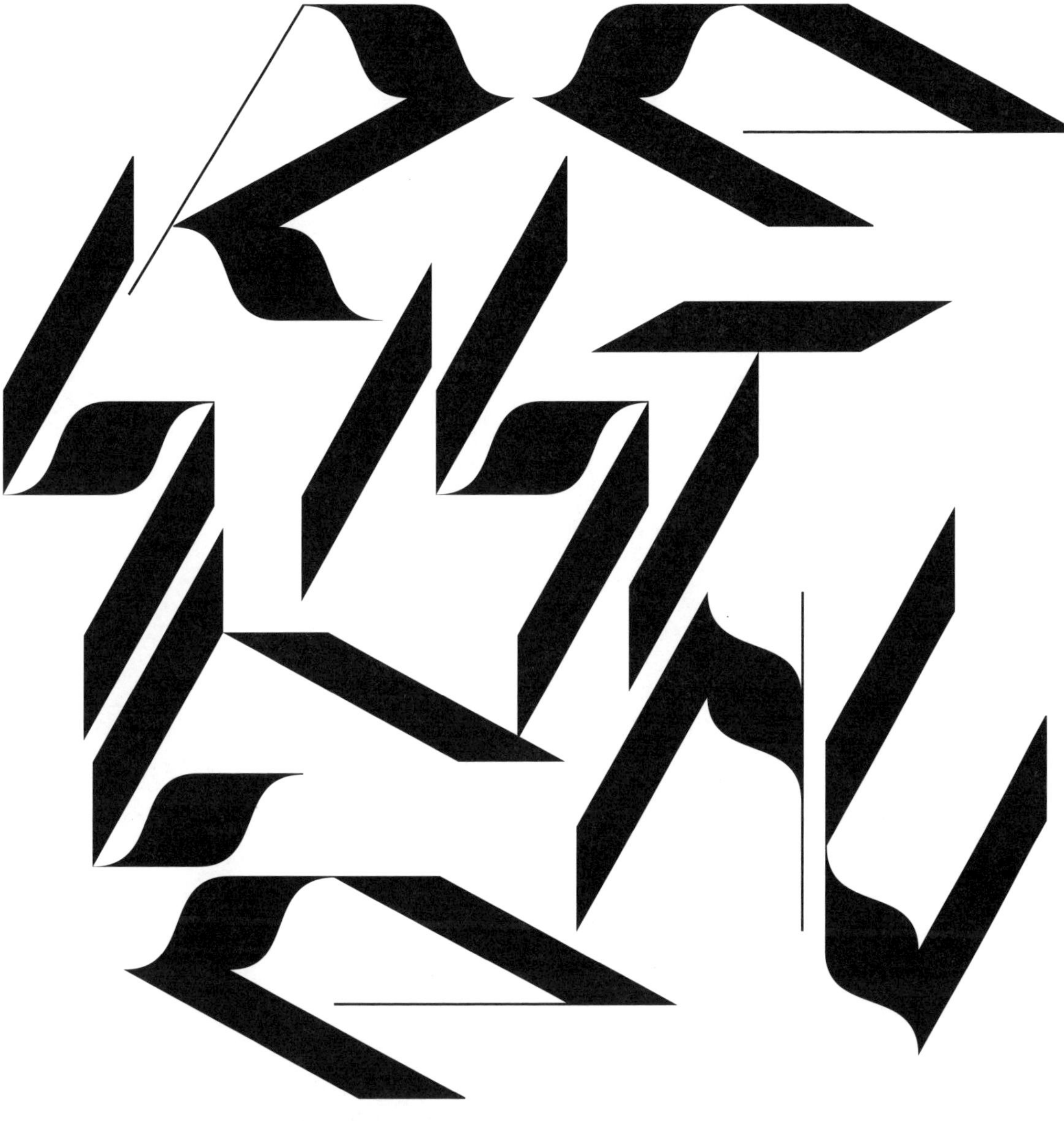

Monstrum
Lorenza Liguori

Monstrum is one of the first typefaces with which I approached font design and was born during a dark period of my life. The typeface develops on pointed and angular shapes and falls into a perfectly square shape. The result is deliberately aggressive and the sensations it transmits are very acute. The use for which it was made concerns dark graphic contexts, but it can also be used in completely different contexts, thanks to its easily adaptable corners.

Classification
Experimental

Styles
New Dark

Release
2019

Contact
@lorenza.liguori
behance.net/lollalig

Character overview on page 256

Mycela
Peter Roeleveld

Glyphs are nice individuals and are always in relation with other characters. In this experiment, I want to take this a step further by creating an endless amount of ligatures when typing. In Mycela, the notion of beauty doesn't rely on a single character as an individual, but more on a combination of characters that make it beautiful together. Mycela gets her name from Mycelium, which is the vegetative part of a fungus or fungus-like bacterial colony, consisting of branching thread-like hyphae. It can either appear so tiny that it can't be seen or grow thousands of acres big. Similar to the fungus, you can grow words in an infinite amount of characters and still keep them connected in this typeface.

Classification
Serif

Styles
Regular

Release
2020

Contact
peterroeleveld.com
@peter_roeleveld

Character overview on page 257

MYCELIA

Sounds Like The Earth is Shaking. Blood Sweat And Tears Dripping.

N—E
Alex Ortiga

N—E is an experimental font whose shapes are inspired by GAN generated forms and meshes. Its glyphs are meant to be used to create abstract shapes or in a decorative/iconographic way. N—E aesthetic wants to evoke the sign of a set of glyphs coming from an ancient and lost future, the hieroglyphs of a forgotten alien civilization. This idea is exploited to devise a new form of communication design where the text becomes an integrated figurative element within the rest of the environment/composition, and no longer just an element to communicate the content of information through syntax. N—E was conceived as a logotype for the sci-fi book "New Economy" written by Alex Ortiga with the aid of an "artificial intelligence", the 1558M language processing model.

Classification
Display

Styles
Regular

Release
2020

Contact
alexortiga.com
@sy____in

Nero Alto
Mateo Broillet

The design of Nero Alto has been inspired by graffiti excavated from Pompeii since the 1800s, vernacular calligraphic gestures from the Roman era and contemporary influences. The design is structured around a sharp and geometric construction while being slightly odd and off. At first caps-only and only destined for banners and posters of a theatre in Amsterdam, the typeface slowly evolved with the addition of lowercase letters, numerous ligatures, and an italic version in the making. Despite being thin, Nero Alto is well suited for display and web use. It can also be used as a text typeface for an uncanny result.

Classification
Display Serif

Styles
Thin

Release
2019

Contact
mateobroillet.ch
@atelieramb

Character overview on page 259

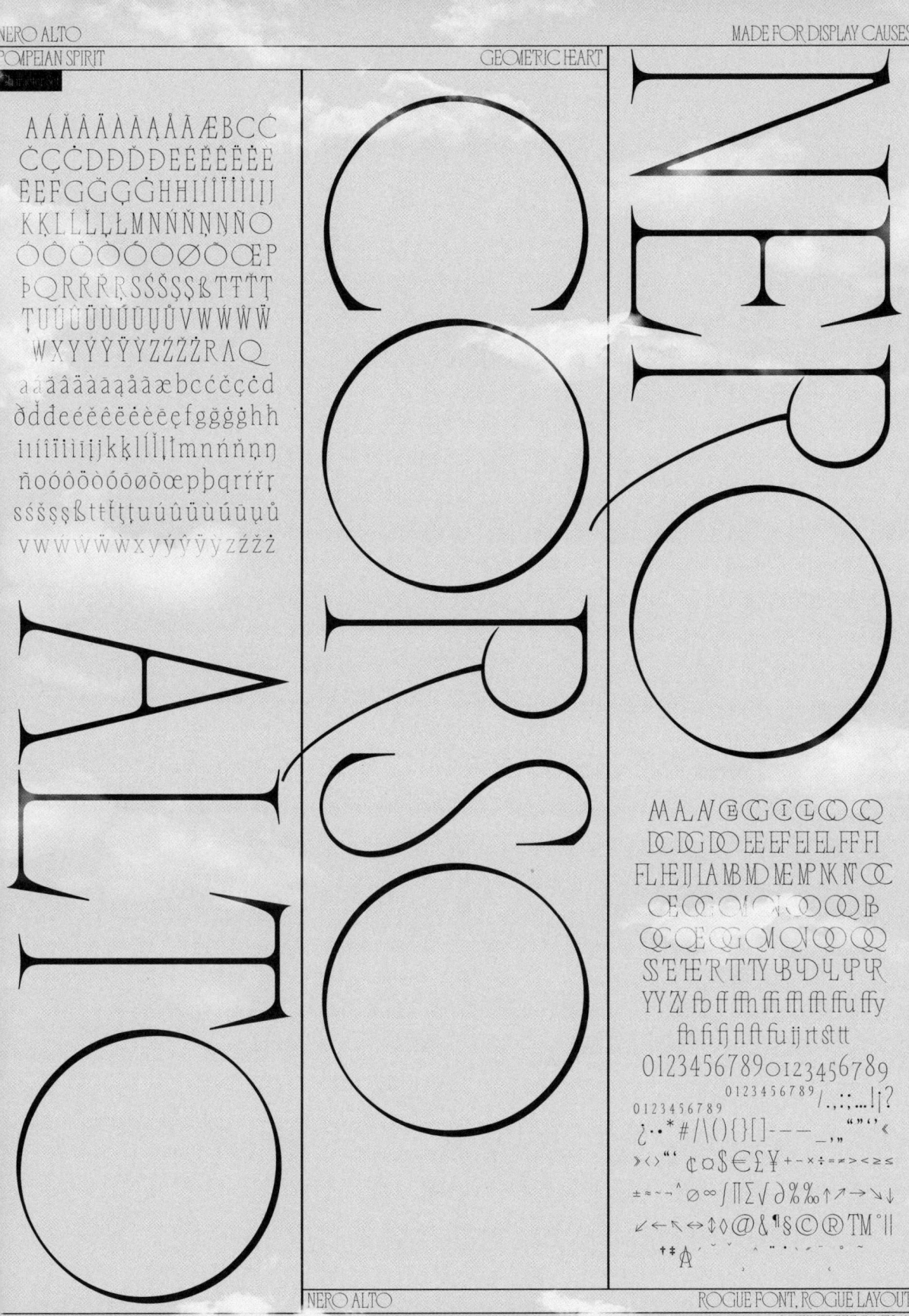

Netbus
Virgile Flores

Vogue type with a twist. Netbus is a straightforward high-contrast didone that combines a rigid geometric & squarish drawing with subtle oddities and a contemporary touch. It covers the Latin Extended Character overview and is available for print and web. Netbus is the very first release of the Trojan Type Factory, a typographic foundry merging elements and references from greek mythology and malware programs. Its name is a reference to a software program for remotely controlling a Microsoft Windows computer system over a network.

Classification
Didone

Styles
Display

Release
2019

Contact
virgileflores.com
@virgileflores

Character overview on page 260

&SLÆKEN

Netbus

@virgileflores 2019

New Diane Script
Paul Bergès

New Diane Script is a new version—or a demolished interpretation—of the ITC Edwardian Script, a calligraphic font designed by Edward Benguiat in 1994. The letters of the font were drawn to create the appearance of true handwriting, they try to imitate human writing. In the New Diane Script, the hand is replaced by a software, the original manual gesture software, therefore the original manual gesture becomes a digital one. Each letter is carefully modified / transformed with the same repetitive mechanical movement. The process is performed almost unconsciously and automatically to recall the habit of handwriting. The result of these transformations gave rise to this hybrid character between a script and an illustrative and almost illegible display font.

Classification
Neo-Script

Styles
Regular

Release
2019

Contact
bergespaul.contact@gmail.com
@begia__

Character overview on page 261

In the New Diane Script, the hand is replaced by a software,
the original manual gesture therefore becomes a digital gesture.

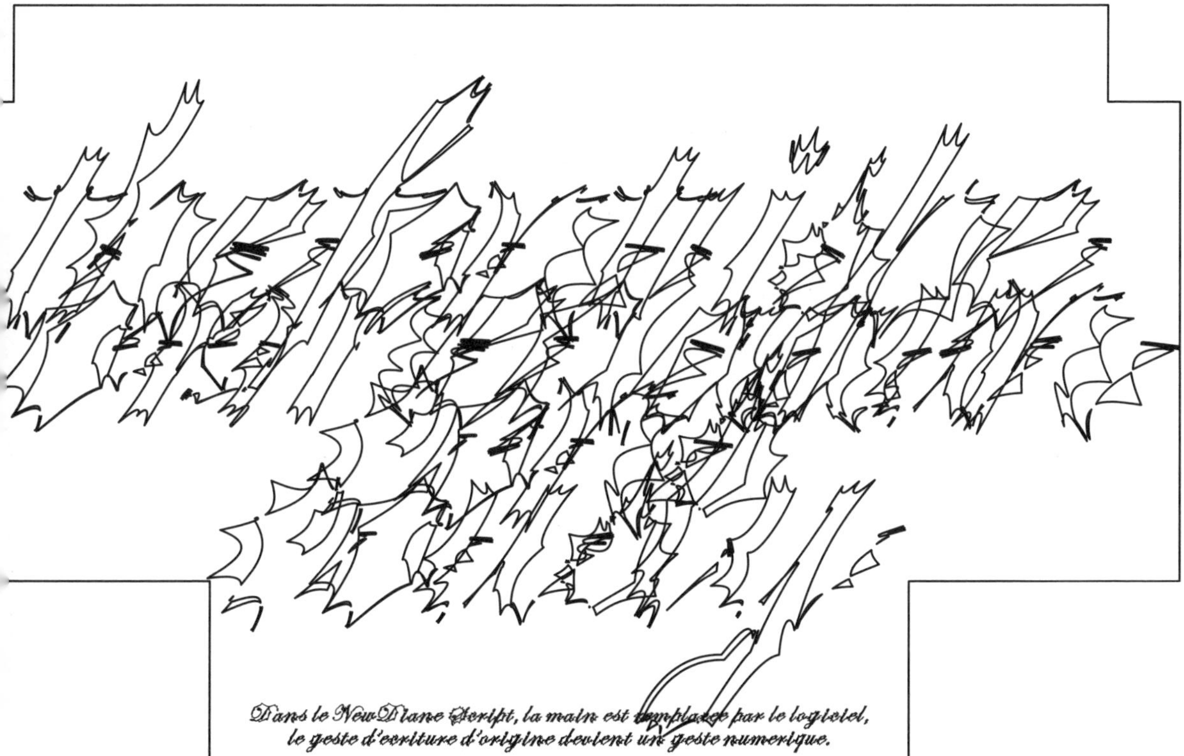

Dans le New Diane Script, la main est remplacée par le logiciel,
le geste d'écriture d'origine devient un geste numérique.

New Peace
Panama Papers Office

Timur Si-Qin, an American contemporary artist, reached out to us to collaborate for his upcoming exposition "Take Me, I Love You" (von ammon co gallery, Washington DC, USA). In a broad sense, our mission was to enrich his artistic branding project's graphical language through typography and layout. This is an atypical assignment because of the nature of our input. Within art shows, graphic design work usually focuses on promoting the artworks and related events. In this precise case, the typographical work we did directly takes place at the core of an installation. New Peace is an allegory of nature in a commercial frame. We considered duality as an important aspect during the process. The font has an organic, calligraphic side as well as a mechanic side that relates to the rigor of academic type design. The design process itself followed the same dichotomy as it was a constant back and forth between analog manual drawing and digital standardization.

Classification
Display

Styles
Regular

Release
2020

Contact
@ppoffice.paris
panamapapersoffice.com

Character overview on page 262

OPEN PRAYER

I PRAY FOR STRENGHT LIKE THE TREE
I PRAY FOR TIME LIKE THE MOUNTAIN
I PRAY FOR FORGIVENESS LIKE THE RIVER
I PRAY FOR WISDOM LIKE THE MOTHER

I AM ALREADY THERE

NF Object
Sophia Brinkgerd

The base of NF Object is a creative process that is driven purely by the interest in form making and visually exploring impressions of our everyday environment. Supported by Kathleen and Christopher Sleboda, the class "Newly Formed" at Rhode Island School of Design had this philosophy at its core: A design approach that creates form first and tells a story through shape, color and composition. During the first weekly task, three typefaces were created based on the terms "System", "Found Object" and "Variable". As a variable font, NF Object unites all of those characteristics with its quirky and playful nature. The width and proportion of the letters can be altered variably, with the letters nesting nicely into the white space. Its boldness reminded me of expressive but simple and functional graphics that are found on construction sites or the graphic style in which handicraft enterprises are usually branded.

Classification
Display Variable

Styles
A
B

Release
N/A

Contact
hey@sophiabrinkgerd.com
sophiabrinkgerd.com
@sophiabrinkgerd

Character overview on page 263

Nine
Raphaël De La Morinerie

This font was designed during a one week workshop. The brief was to draw a stencil font and use it to design posters. As I needed a framework to design good posters, I decided to work with the '90s 2000s graphic aesthetics. I designed a modular typeface whose shapes come from the LCD display. It was a way to draw sharp and agressive forms. To define its proportions I added an extra constraint. I wanted to have a monospace font to compose words and letters on a super rational grid. It is then possible to abstract letters and to compose them as patterns.

Classification
Display

Styles
Regular

Release
2019

Contact
raphaeldelamorinerie.fr
@raph____ael

Character overview on page 264

type is shaped by technology

Noir Serif
Lucas Hesse, Paul Schmidt, Malte Schwenker

The characters are based on a combination of sharp serifs and soft curves. The typeface was build very systematically and thus never claimed to be suitable for everyday use or easy to read. The focus was to rather create something special. We experimented with different forms and their combinations by explaining different known letterforms to each other and then, without knowing the original, drawing them. This resulted in a wide range of wired glyphs. From the final building blocks, consisting of rectangles, triangles and various fixed curves, all letters were put together without compromise. This created the often wired but systematic character of the typeface.

Classification
Serif

Styles
Regular

Release
2018

Contact
lucas-hesse.de
@_hesselucas
schmidt-paul.eu
@schmidtpaul.eu
malteschwenker.de
@malteschwenker

Character overview on page 265

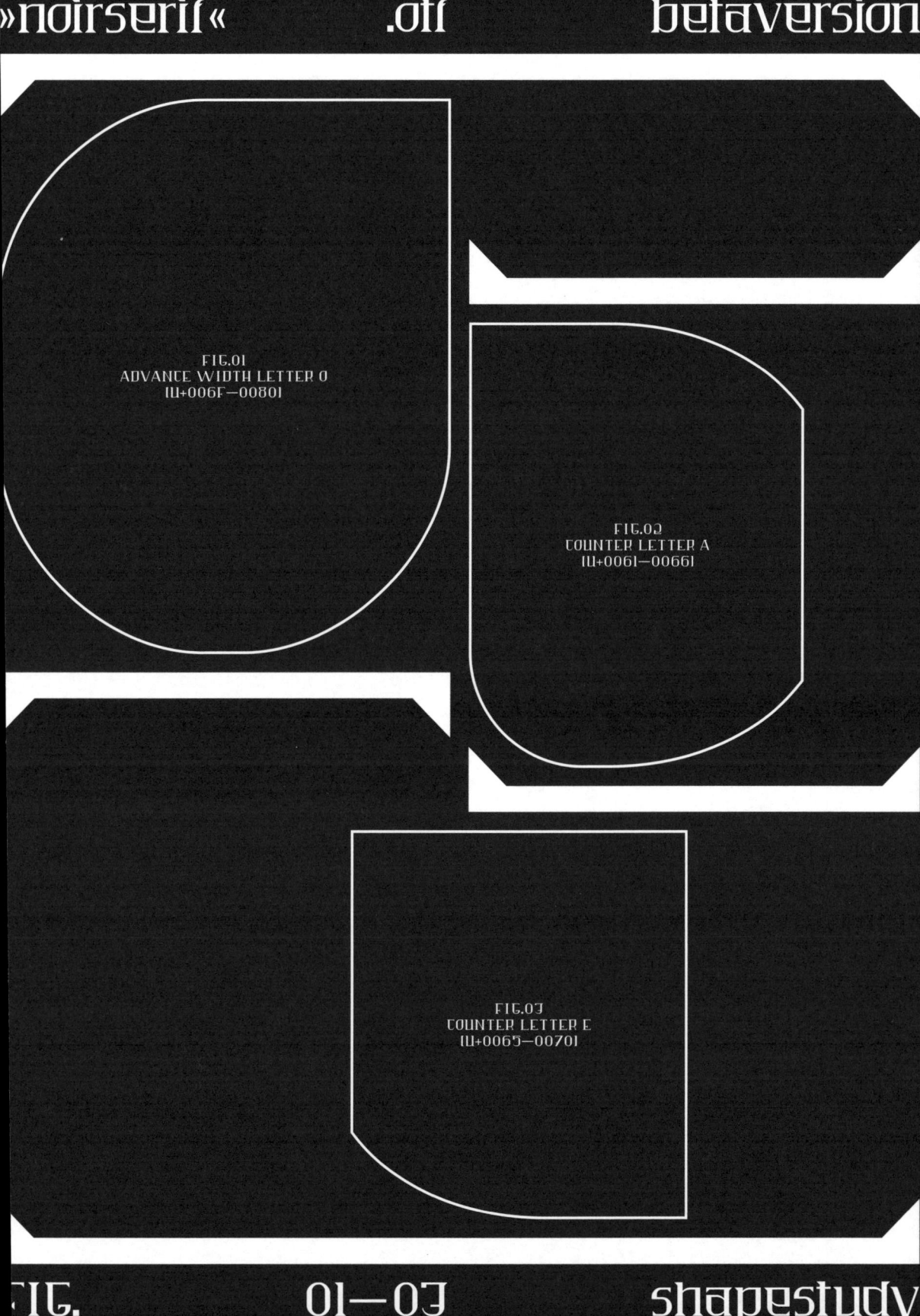

FIG.01
ADVANCE WIDTH LETTER O
[U+006F—0080]

FIG.02
COUNTER LETTER A
[U+0061—0066]

FIG.03
COUNTER LETTER E
[U+0065—0070]

FIG. 01—03 shapestudy

Oliver
Ishar Hawkins

Oliver.otf is a typeface developed by Ishar Hawkins and Fog Man in 2018. It aims to combine the dark and ominous aesthetics of gothic type with the soulless uniformity of digital aesthetics. There has been a revival or resurgence of gothic and medieval type in the past few years and Oliver hopes to exist as a middle man between the two worlds of digital and medieval. What does a digital typeface look like in a gothic landscape? What does a gothic typeface look like in a digital landscape?

Classification
Display

Styles
Regular

Release
2019

Contact
@isharhawkins

Character overview on page 266

Omelett
Bedow Design

Omelett Display was initially drawn for a Swedish company making vintage photo booths. Its name derives from the popular photographer's cue 'Say Cheese', which is 'Say Omelette' in Swedish. The result is a posing typeface, mirroring people's tendency to strike a different pose for each of the four frames on a typical photo strip. The typeface has four alternate glyphs per letterform to represent the four frames on a typical photo strip. Instead of having different styles or additional italics, Omelett Display has four poses. Each letter has a frame that further references the frames on a photo strip.

Classification
Display

Styles
Pose 1
Pose 2
Pose 3
Pose 4

Release
2018

Contact
bedow.se
@bedowdesign

Character overview on page 267

Omelett

Once Again
Han Gao

It's an attempt to challenge the technique and skills I have learnt in the last few years. I went back to creating spacing and structures simply by using the basic line itself. I did it in an extreme way, way more extreme than I expected. In the process, I was fascinated with how much influence it could make to simply change the thickness, direction, or corner of the strokes. I basically just played with the turns and round corners to make balanced space by trying lots of possible paths for each letter. It's not only an aesthetic finish for each letter, but also about building the alphabet under a strict grid system and let the letters work as whole.

Classification
Futuristic Sans Serif

Styles
Extended

Release
2019

Contact
@workbyworks

Character overview on page 268

Ornamentum
Hugo Jourdan

At the beginning, Ornamentum was just a titling for a poster that I did for the event "Une Saison Graphique 2019". After this event, some persons asked me if this typeface was available and motivated me to design the complete Latin alphabet. Ornamentum has been designed to be used as much for composing text as for creating ornaments. You can use letters in isolation to build your own ornaments or together with a special OpenType feature that I coded to create ornamental lines. Ornamentum is available in three styles : light, regular and bold. The glyphset includes capitals, numbers and few punctuations.

Classification
Techno Futurist

Styles
Regular

Release
2019

Contact
@hugojourdan

Character overview on page 269

ABCDEFGHIJKLM
NOPQRSTUVWXYZ

Pandemonium
István Fazekas

Pandemonium is a stencil display typeface designed by István Fazekas, a Budapest-based Hungarian graphic designer. The process of creating Pandemonium started as a school project at Moholy-Nagy University of Art and Design Budapest. The students were given the task of designing a stencil typeface. István, a beginner type designer at the time, decided to create something radically different from the traditional robust stencil fonts. He got inspired by the shapes of fire flames and the curves of handwriting. With its elastic, curling shapes this typeface creates a mysterious, dark atmosphere. This evil vibe helped finding the perfect name for this font. Pandemonium is the capital of hell, "the High Capital, of Satan and his Peers", built by the fallen angels at the suggestion of Mammon at the end of Book I of Paradise Lost by John Milton.

Classification
Stencil

Styles
Regular

Release
2019

Contact
@_fazekas_istvan

Character overview on page 270

Paradoxa
Christos Georgatos

Paradoxa (Παραδόξα) was made as part of my diploma project for my graphic design bachelor in Greece. The typeface was based on the Greek fonts that were produced in Venice during 15th and 16th century. These fonts were full of ligatures and because some of them are still readable in Greek language, I tried to recreate them in Paradoxa. In total, the typeface has over 100 ligatures in every weight. The reason I chose to create this font was because I see all the time beautiful new serif typefaces in Latin and Cyrillic, but almost never in Greek. I tried to fill this gap in the best of my abilities.

Classification
Serif

Styles
Regular
Bold
Black Caps

Release
2020

Contact
chris1996geo@gmail.com
@morg.o.tron

Character overview on page 271

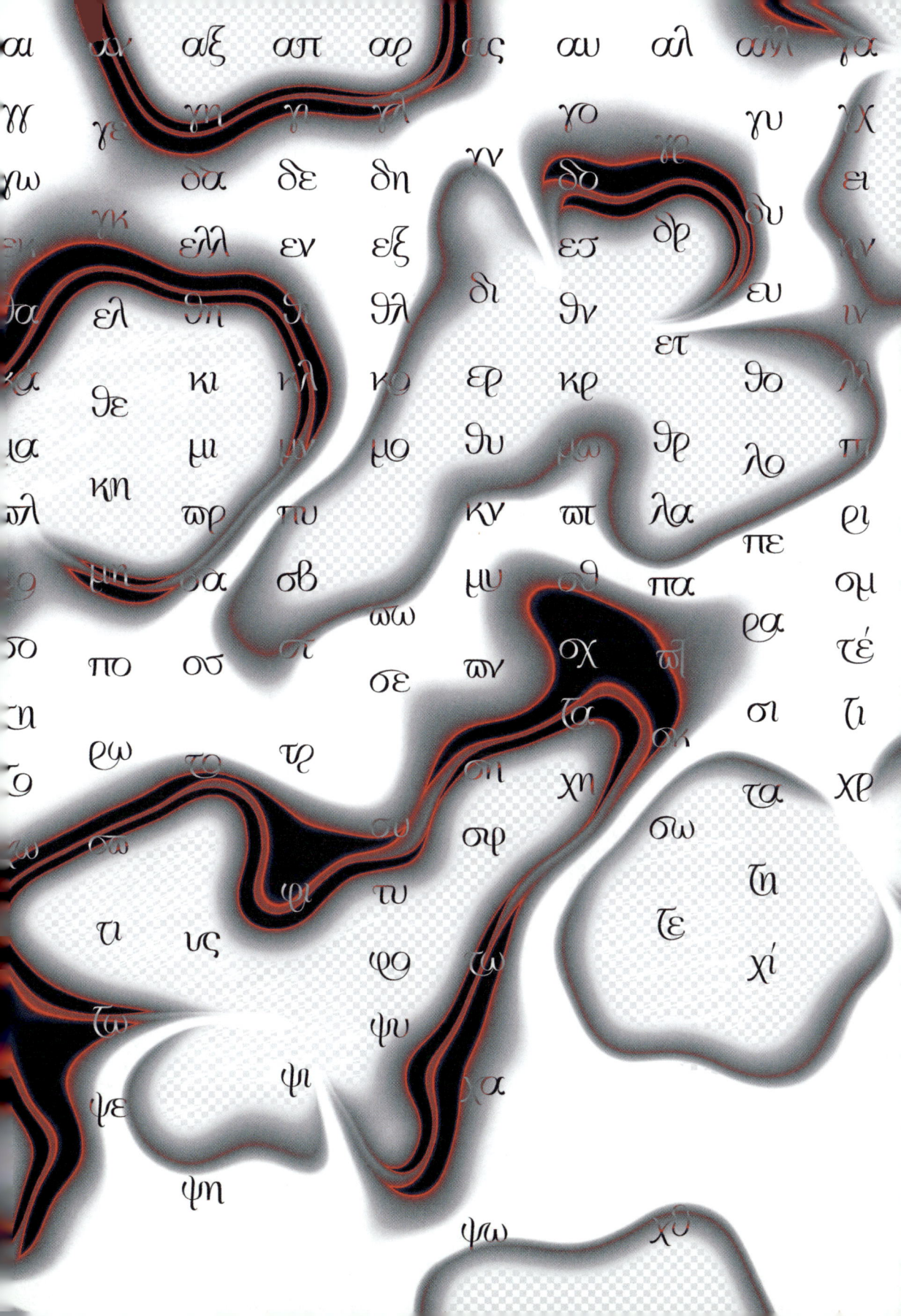

Pentex
Sascha Bente

Pentex derived from an experiment using a correction pen as a writing tool on dark background. Where the hand stops to turn and change directions, dark spots appear and get bigger the longer you stay on the same spot. The Typeface was developed together with Radim Peško at Master Type Design at ECAL. It features a circular and a purely angular set of glyphs.

Classification
Experimental Display

Styles
Skeleton
Inkspot
Regular
Bold
Black

Release
2019

Contact
saschabente.com
@sascha.bente

PIZZERIA ALFABEATO

ABCDEFGHIJKLMNOPQRSTUVWXYZ
CDGOQS—0123456789
*¿!

OFFERTA
DELLA *
SERATA
-1-
APEROL
SWISS
★ SOLI
4,90CHF

OFFERTA
DELLA
SERATA *
-2-
NEGRONI
SBAGLIATO
★ SOLI
7,50CHF

BUON PREZZO!

Phase
Elias Hanzer

Phase, a generative type concept experimenting with variable font technology, is systematically designed with two modular components, which form the base for an infinite number of shapes. Phase can be manipulated in real-time or via sound input (eliashanzer.com/phase). Singular states of the typeface can be downloaded and used for personal and testing purposes.

Classification
Display

Styles
A
B
C
D
E
F
G
H

Release
2018

Contact
eliashanzer.com
hanli.eu
@eliashanzer

Character overview on page 273

Phase
Phase
Phase
Phase
Phase
...

Poster Mono
Lena Karoline Weber

Poster Mono reevaluates the line between graphic design and typography. It treats the data format of a typeface as a possibility to map graphics onto the keyboard interface. Therefore, graphic design is made typable. Poster Mono is based on a square grid which allows the glyphs to merge with one another seamlessly. After creating the shape one likes, they can be stretched to disguise the components used. This encrypted typeface is a tool used to experiment with abstract shapes, encouraging the designer to adapt a new workflow. Randomness and happy accidents play a major role in using this specific typeface as one is typing and creating blindly to a certain extent. Poster Mono is the beginning of a family of monospace graphic fonts, which are all based on the same grid.

Classification
Experimental

Styles
Regular

Release
2019

Contact
lenaweber-design.de
@lenaweber404

Character overview on page 274

Protégé
Paola Bombelli

Protégé is a typeface inspired by two artists: Adolfo Wildt, modernist, and one of his pupils Fausto Melotti, a pioneer of geometric abstraction in Italy. The physiognomy of this typeface comes from the study of the shapes of their sculptures. In the 'Regular' style, serifs, terminals, shoulders, links, they all recall the same curves and shapes of Wildt's aesthetics; sinuous movements, alternating sharp corners and curvilinear forms. The 'Hairline' style develops a geometric monoline that represents an extreme synthesis of the former. The rhythm created visually evokes the alternation of solids and voids typical of Menotti's slender, light sculptures.

Classification
Serif

Styles
Regular
Hairline

Release
N/A

Contact
paolabombelli.com
@p_fulmicotton

Character overview on page 275

Protégé

*t
"La torre
di Babele"

Dem ande -moi tout.

*v
"La battaglia
sul greto"

«Demande-moi une chose,
Pideme alfo. Demande-moi tout
Forse If I see you.»

Fausto Melotti

Rapido GP
János Hunor Vári

Rapido GP is a hommage to the 1980's race car designs and vintage car sticker traditions and a result of experimenting with new letterforms that I started in 2019 with designing a logo for a musician called Baba Aziz. This typeface is a beta still, but already a result of a long journey of experimenting, and redefining some letter shapes especially the capital R. All the characters had been drawn in a specific grid with 6 columns and 5 rows, which are also divided to subcolumns and subrows to provide more space for the playful shapes. In the future, I'm planning to continue experimenting with several things such as ink traps etc. and to release more Styles of the typeface.

Classification
Experimental Display

Styles
Regular

Release
2020

Contact
thispopshitpop.tumblr.com
@thispopshitpop

Character overview on page 276

Rapido

GP Beta

stri7993

GT

motor city ★

sky

nasa

S6

|||||345 rmph mph

oil 2020

RED
Frédéric Jaman, Vrints Kolsteren

Made in collaboration with Vrints Kolsteren at Antwerp, RED is a title font with geometric and pointed terminations influenced by Gothic writing. The alphabet was thought like an auto-initiated project for the football World Cup in Russia in July 2018. This typeface made its first appearance on a flag to support the Belgian national team: The "Red Devils".

Classification
Experimental Display

Styles
Regular

Release
2019

Contact
@frederic_jaman
@vrintskolsteren

Character overview on page 277

RED DEVILS

THIBAUT COURTOIS TOBY ALDERWEIRELD BRANDON MECHELE LEANDER DENDONCKER
JASON DENAYER AXEL WITSEL KEVIN DE BRUYNE YOURI TIELEMANS ROMELU LUKAKU EDEN HAZARD
YANNICK FERREIRA CARRASCO SIMON MIGNOLET MATZ SELS DRIES MERTENS ELIAS COBBAUT
THORGAN HAZARD DIVOCK ORIGI HANS VANAKEN DENNIS PRAET CHRISTIAN BENTEKE TIMOTHY CASTAGNE
YARI VERSCHAEREN MICHY BATSHUAYI HENDRIK VAN CROMBRUGGE THOMAS VERMAELEN
DEDRYCK BOYATA NACER CHADLI MAXIME LESTIENNE LEANDRO TROSSARD

RED ROOD ROT ROUGE

Renzo
Robert Radziejewski

Renzo explores the boundaries of readability based on the concept of unity and separation. Renzo comes in three cuts which are defined as "United", "Univided" and "Divided". The cuts don't describe the weight, but rather the way the letters change their form by dividing them into separate shapes. As the shapes of the letters drift apart, they become less recognizable and words turn into abstract structures. In the "United" cut all letterparts are being held together so that the letters appear as singular entities. The "Divided" cut blurs the line between a readable letter and an abstract structure. The "Univided" cut has line-like interspaces within the letter-shapes and acts as a state between the two extremes. The variable cut allows individual adjustment of the shape separation.

Classification
Display

Styles
United
Univided
Divided

Release
2021

Contact
radzie.de
@robert.radziejewski

Character overview on page 278

Romie
Margot Lévêque

I learned type design by doing calligraphy on layers. Once I decided to vectorise one of my drawings and develop the full typeface on glyphs, I designed Romie. The serifs of Romie are very specific. They remind me of the '60s fashion, because this era offered a new silhouette to women and broke the codes with new cuts, colors and lengths. In 2018, I have not seen contemporary typefaces that used historical serifs like Romie's. In November 2019, when I was a designer at Pentagram in NYC, the designer Lorenzo Fanton saw one of my files opened on my computer. He asked me for the name of the typeface! I explained to him that it was one of mine and soon the collaboration started. This is how Romie Ligatures was born!

Classification
Serif

Styles
Regular
Ligatures

Release
2019

Contact
margotleveque.com
@margot.leveque

Character overview on page 279

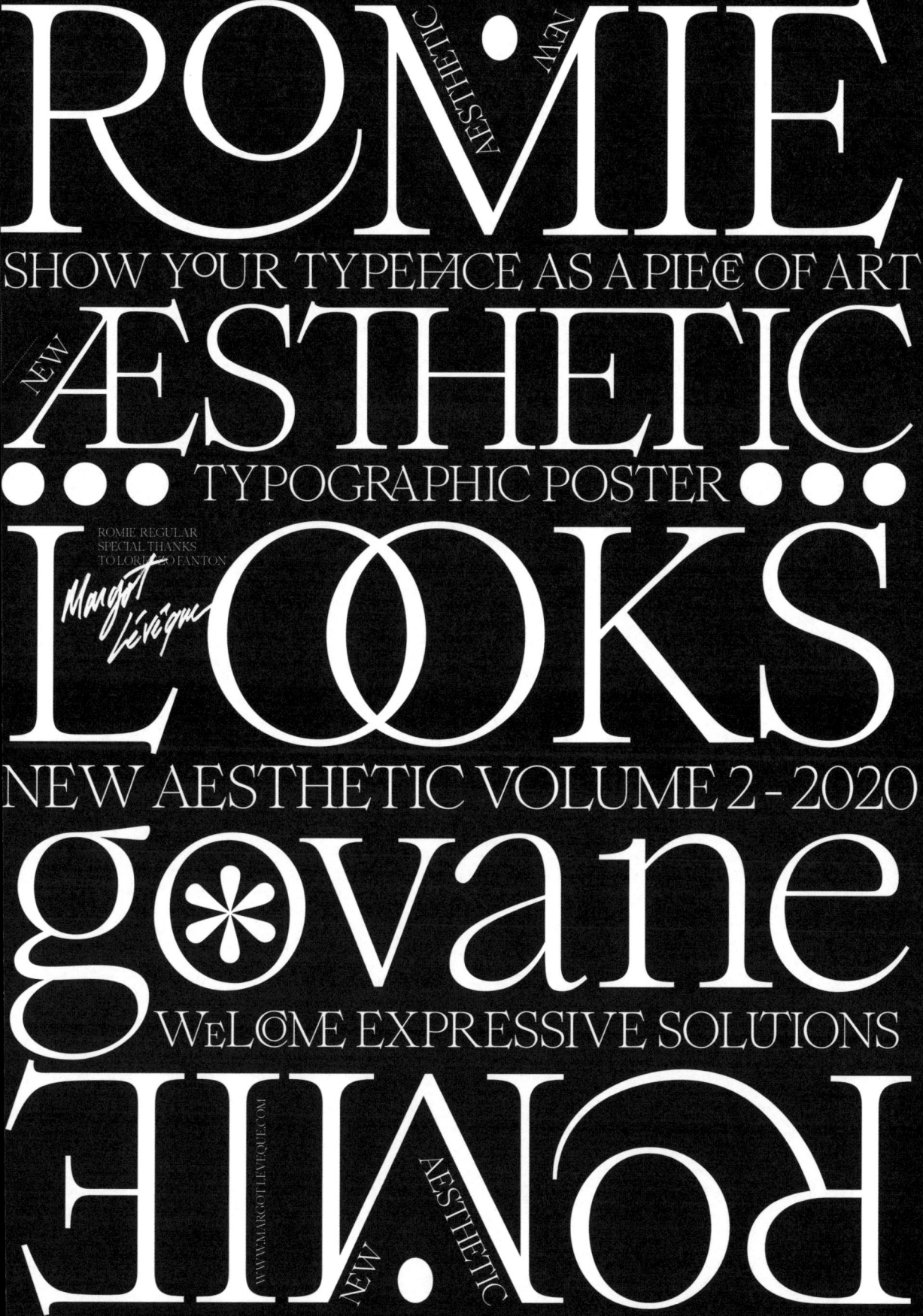

Rosdar
Daan Rietbergen

Rosdar is a grid-based typeface designed in quarantine during the COVID-19 pandemic. When I design a typeface, I work with one strong basic principle. This principle determines the graphic language and the rules I impose on myself sometimes outweigh the legibility. In this case, there is an undulating movement in all the characters. Specific parts are exaggerated, for example the belly of the lowercase a. The typeface is not consciously inspired by other languages or scripts, but many people see similarities with languages that I did not know, such as Armenian, Cambodian and South Indian scripts such as Malayalam and Telugu.

Classification
Grid-Based

Styles
Regular

Release
2020

Contact
daanrietbergen.com
@daan_rietbergen

Character overview on page 280

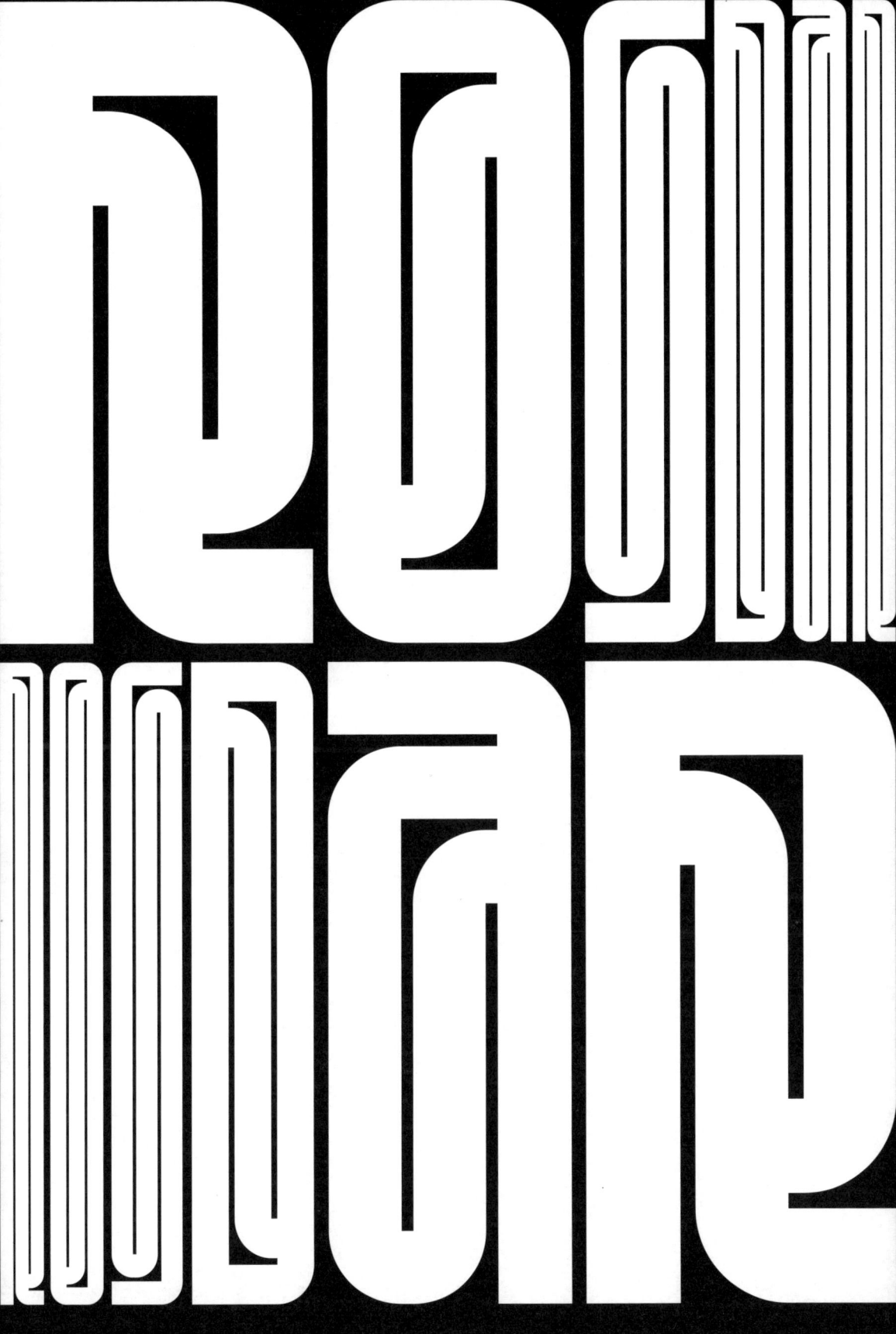

Scotch Genovese
Scott Vander Zee

With lineal ties to the Scotch Roman typeface classification, I've named this one Scotch Genovese. The De Vinne typeface—designed by Gustav F. Schroeder in 1890 and named after the American printer, author, and typographer Theodore Low De Vinne—is among one of my favorite Scotch Roman typefaces. Thinking about the origins of naming, typography's debt to Italian inscribed lettering (specifically Roman), and given my partner and in-laws are from Genova, I simply liked the idea of playing off notions of family, naming, proximity, history, and context in order to push an "antiquated" traditional type style/classification into the contemporary type scene. And Scotch Genovese was initiated.

Classification
Serif

Styles
Display
Display Italic
Book
Book Italic

Release
2020

Contact
scott@scott-vanderzee.com
scott-vanderzee.com
@s.vd.z

Character overview on page 281

E●STATE INSIEME SAGRA

NUMERO

XXI

17.7
V

18.7
S

19.7
D

PROGRAMMA
ROBY BOLOGNA

PROGRAMMA
MGNOLI & MESSINA

PROGRAMMA
ASD MASTER BALLET —
SERATA DISCO
CON ANIMAZIONE

●●INFO

SEDE
CIRCOLO CONFIDENZA
SAN BARTOLOMEO
VIA N.S. DEL SOCCORSO
16039 SESTRI LEVANTE (GE)

PARCHEGGIO
AMPI PARCHEGGI LUNGO LA
STRADA PARCO

MENÜ: VEGETARIANO
TESTAROLI AL PESTO
TAGLIATELLE AI FUNGHI
POLPETTONE FAGIOLINI E PATATE
VERDURE ALLA PIASTRA
TIRAMISU
VINO NOSTRALINO E BIRRA

PROGRAMMA
APERTURA STANDS GASTRONOMICI ORE 19:30
DALLE ORE 21:00 SERATE DANZANTI
(VEDI SOPRA)

Sentinel
Eric Lish

The process of crafting Sentinel began as an exploration between digital and calligraphic characteristics to develop a typeface that felt futuristic while acknowledging past methods of typographic construction. Angles that protrude from selected letters give agency to the dynamic relationship of space between glyphs while reinterpreting their shape to an alien quality. The exaggeration of these angles allows Sentinel to reminisce on blackletter pen logic and combines this contrast with the rigidity of LCD/LED typographic structure of digital interfaces. Sentinel's thin strokes and height give a feeling of monolithic proportions that coalesce with its sharp edges to give it a precise presence.

Classification
Experimental

Styles
Regular

Release
2020

Contact
ericlish.com
@lisheric

Character overview on page 282

Shinobi
Kazuhiro Aihara

Shinobi is inspired by the historical Japanese spy/ninja. He moves silently, is flexible and finishes his missions. Nobody notices them. The font is like a ninja jumping over the wall. At the same time, I try to express nervousness with the irregular streamline form. I have flown around between legible and illegible on purpose. That is exactly Shinobi's existence.

Classification
Handwriting

Styles
Regular

Release
2020

Contact
shunto-sha.com
@shuntoheyog

Character overview on page 283

Shokoofeh
Leonhard Laupichler

Afghanistan, the largest war zone in the world, is characterized by destruction. I try to juxtapose this deconstruction that is happening in Afghanistan with the creation that can be found in its vegetation. Afghanistan has diverse and beautiful landscapes such as unique flora which served as my inspiration. This examination of war and vegetation results in an experiment on expressive typography. I created alienated and destroyed forms based on trees, bushes and flowers that are native in Afghanistan, and digitized them. From these forms I developed a glyph set including characters from A–Z.

Classification
Cut Out

Styles
Creation
Destruction

Release
2020

Contact
leonhard@leonhardlaupichler.com
leonhardlaupichler.com
@leonhardlaupichler

Character overview on page 284

Sinistre
Jules Durand

Sinistre was conceived over the last 3 years. His character has evolved to become stronger and bigger, the glyphset is still growing, each time of his life is marked on a dedicated stylistic set. I like to tell the stories behind my fonts, perhaps this is too long for now, so, if you would like to know more, I invite you to look for A Tale of Type at the dedicated website. Let's go back to Sinistre: It is inspired by the Roman architecture, some Gothic ornaments, organic ligatures and weird alternates from another age. Looking at manuscripts from Charlemagne's reign, I was dazzled by the freshness of Caroline's curves, craziness of initials and mysticism of some skilled monks. So I did a secret weight of Sinistre, called Carolus Magnus, which is much more ornamented, sophisticated, and yet very privy & cryptic.

Classification
Neon Uncial

Styles
Saint

Release
2020

Contact
julesdurand.xyz
@lazy_dog.ttf

Character overview on page 285

DUNGEON

ROMÄNISCH

OPEN:HAUS

LOVECRAFT

MEDIÆVAL

ANTIQUA

PROTO:UNCIAL

LATEGOTHIQUE

Le Chevalier du
Château Maudit
Il cavaliere del
castello maledetto
NAZGUL
COSTA
1959

The Warlock of
Firetop Mountain
Le Sorcier de la
Montagne de Feu
Steve Jackson &
Ian Livingstone
1982

Sissi Display
Fabian Maier-Bode

Sissi Display was developed during my sabbatical I took in Milano, Italy. At some point, my ex-wife and I were watching the movie Sissi with Romy Schneider from 1955. Inspired by the dresses and the furniture I started to play around with modular shapes with a strong visual relation to this movie. One day, I realized that the first letters I drew had some very interesting details. This kept me motivated to finish Sissi. What's interesting about this display typeface? The shapes are beautiful and dangerous at the same time. It challenges its readers and surprises with a lot strange details.

Classification
Modern Modular Blackletter

Styles
Regular

Release
2020

Contact
fabianmaierbode.de
@fabianmaierbode

Character overview on page 286

dass ich als ich
ein und zwei ist
dass ich als ich
drei und vier ist
dass ich als ich
wieviel zeigt sie
dass ich als ich
tickt und tackt sie
dass ich als ich
fünf und sechs ist
dass ich als ich
sieben acht ist
dass ich als ich
wenn sie steht sie
dass ich als ich
wenn sie geht sie
dass ich als ich
neun und zehn ist
dass ich als ich
elf und zwölf ist.

Sometimes Times
Samuel Glen Hughes

Sometimes Times was Boulevard LAB's debut serif typeface, designed by Samuel Glen Hughes. Sometimes Times is an experimental typeface reshaping the essence of the classic Times serifs without all the bulk. With its initial release in late 2019, published solely in single light weight, the result was more display style, making it ideal when set in large, pushing the typeface to be seen on the likes of posters, headlines, etc. The approach to create a new unique serif for the modern day led to the creation of a contemporary eccentric feeling and distinctive sleek, elegant look of Sometimes Times.

Classification
Serif

Styles
Regular
Italic

Release
2019

Contact
boulevardlab.com
@boulevard.lab

Character overview on page 287

TIME OF A TEMPO— RARY NATURE

SoundShape XP01
Giuseppe Tangaro

SoundShape XP01 is an experimental all caps and monospaced typeface designed during the 365Type Challenge. The goal of this thematic challenge launched on Instagram by 365typefaces at the end of 2019 was to promote experimental typefaces and, in particular, representatives of sound shapes for the purpose of creating a real, multiple, contemporary and experimental sound alphabet. SoundShape typeface was created with the desire to reproduce the letters of the alphabet based on two different shapes: sinusoidal and square shapes. These two structures refer to the square waves and sine waves of an oscillator inside a drum machine. Oscillator's task is to generate a cyclic voltage variation then repeated in time defined waveform. The final outcome is a set of typefaces that are intertwined with each other, an alphabet that generates complex patterns visually and brings us back to sound waves.

Classification
Monospace

Styles
Curved
Square

Release
2020

Contact
guise.philos@gmail.com
@giuseppe_tangaro

Character overview on page 288

SpiritualRunes
Sophia Krasomil

SpiritualRunes is one out of two typefaces I created for my bachelor project called "entwined", which is dealing with the connections, interdependence, and similarities of technology and spirituality. During the design process, my main source of inspiration was magical symbols, spells, and rituals. SpiritualRunes is made out of strong and spiky shapes that are creating a mystical and eerie atmosphere, providing a glimpse into a transcendental sphere.

Classification
Display

Styles
Regular

Release
2020

Contact
@sophia_krasomil

 Character overview on page 289

Splitter
Arthur Schwarz

Splitter is a typeface inspired by a baseball's spin when pitched. When a baseball is pitched, the goal is not to be hit by the batter. Thus the pitcher knows several ways of throwing the ball in order to trick the hitter. In the end, it's difficult to tell where the baseball is landing. Splitter is a reverse contrast typeface with fast curves and contrasted strokes. It has an unintuitive calligraphic style in order to get closer to the 'baseball pitch' idea. Its non connecting ending strokes make it flavourful and very unique.

Classification
Reverse Contrast Grotesque

Styles
Regular

Release
2020

Contact
arthurschwarz.ch
@arthur_schwarz

Character overview on page 290

Breaks down suddenly...

...before reaching plate!

HOMERUN!

Tabi
Carolina Festa

Tabi is a display type family of two extremes. It started as an academic project by Carolina Festa from the assignment named "Type Family Out Of Comfort"; it was later released with TDFoundry in November 2019. The first sketches were inspired by a sculpture of Swedish artist Lars Englund and the design of both styles was centred on the concept of dualism (Darkness/Light Form/Contraform Readable/Enigmatic). This resulted in the unapologetic Super style, which is meant to create a bridge between functional type and cryptic illustrative forms or symbols. Tabi Super is disruptive and bold, its shapes seem inflated and the concept of functional inktrap is exceeded and exaggerated. The clean Regular style is neutral in aesthetic and much lighter. Ideal to compliment or mix with the Super style.

Classification
Display

Styles
Regular
Super

Release
2019

Contact
@carolahaine
carolahaine.tumblr.com

Character overview on page 291

Techniquæ Antiqua
Antonio D'Elisiis

During a workshop directed by Radim Peško at ECAL, I took an experimental approach to type design. The project was looking for typographic shapes that are unconventional and extremely stimulating. Starting from a text about the technique intended as technologies through the ages have changed the mental structures of the human being, I designed typographic shapes passing through different tools. From the use of the freehand sketch, through the experimentation of 3D shapes, up to the final sketch of a few letters, which summarized the whole experimentation path made in the previous days. The shapes from the workshop later served as a starting point for the typeface. Techniquae Antiqua shows a strong stylistic reference to the Etruscan writing system, while the shapes are within the limits of legibility. This was translated into two versions of letter forms, which can be interchanged to make the typeface extremely playful and modular.

Classification
Experimental Grotesk

Styles
Regular

Release
2020

Contact
hi@antoniodelisiis.it
antoniodelisiis.it
@antoniodelisiis

Character overview on page 292

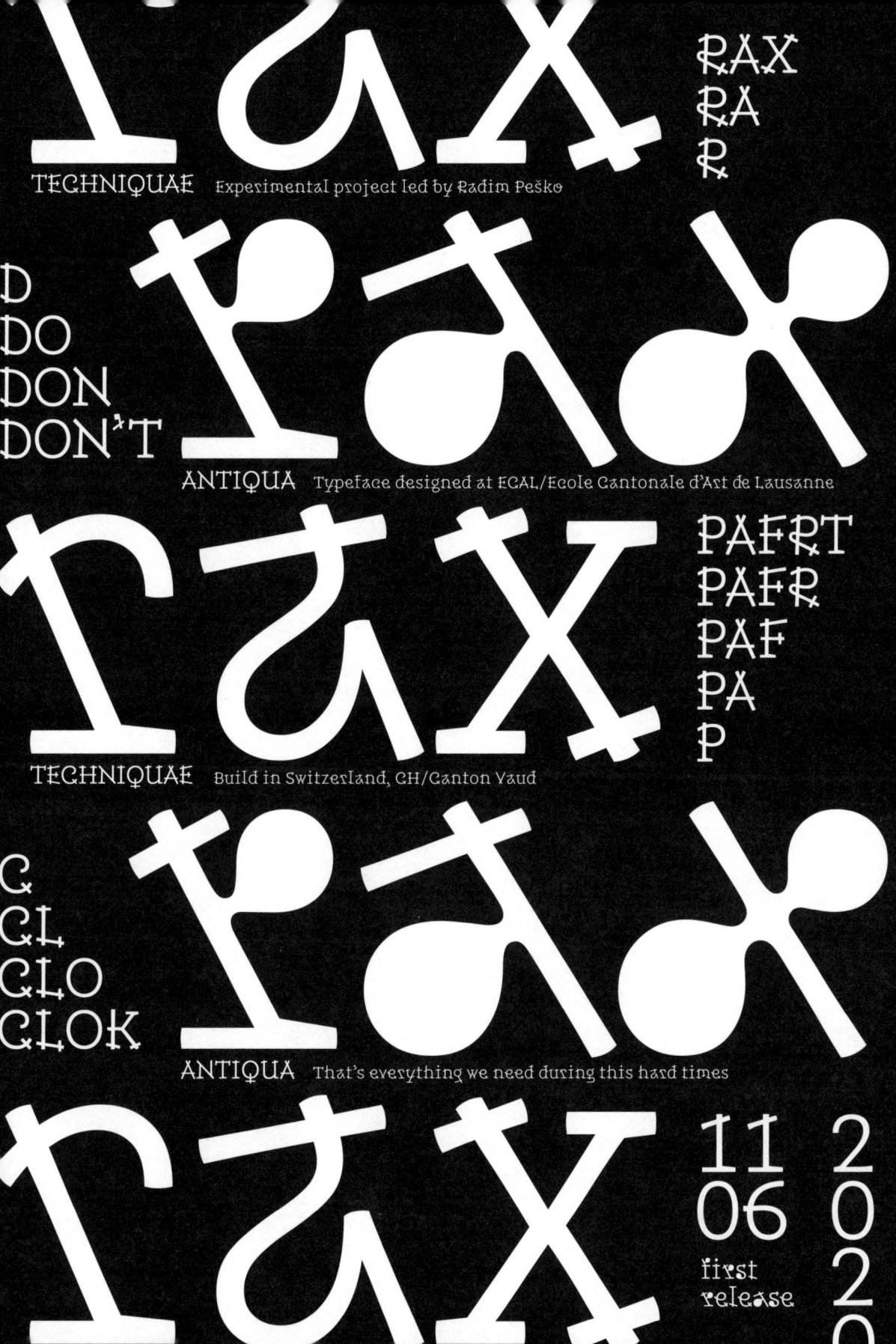

RAX
RA
R

TECHNIQUAE   Experimental project led by Radim Peško

D
DO
DON
DON'T

ANTIQUA   Typeface designed at ECAL/Ecole Cantonale d'Art de Lausanne

PAFRT
PAFR
PAF
PA
P

TECHNIQUAE   Build in Switzerland, CH/Canton Vaud

C
CL
CLO
CLOK

ANTIQUA   That's everything we need during this hard times

11
06

first
release

2
0
2
0

Till
Pauline Le Pape

Till Melted is the new member of the Till family, which has been in development since 2017 and started with Till Normal. Till is inspired by engraved typography and their specific ligatures—observed in Amsterdam, Paris and everywhere in between. Grounded in its historical references, Till also aims to achieve a contemporary feeling. Till Melted is playing around with the characteristics of Till Normal, a counter intuitive version of engraved roman typefaces. It's a soft and curvy yet light version of it.

Classification
Serif

Styles
Normal
Melted

Release
2020

Contact
paulinelepape.com
@paulinelpape

Character overview on page 293

TILL MELTED

AOP

FOURME D'AMBERT
C A N T A L
BLEU D'AUVERGNE
R E B L O C H O N
M O R B I E R
E P O I S S E S
MONT D'OR
B R O C C I U
M A R O I L L E S
BRIE DE MEAUX
CAMEMBERT DE NORMANDIE
PONT L'ÉVÊQUE
R O Q U E F O R T
CHABICHOU DU POITOU
OSSAU IRATY
R O C A M A D O U R

TpRawkost
Dr. Martin Lorenz, TwoPoints.Net

TpRawkost is the result of an experiment trying to make a display font with only two elements. I love these experiments. They are like a game to me. There are clear rules, but there is also room for creativity to find an interesting solution for each of the letters. Legibility is not my main concern when working for myself. I do not need to sell a product. I am mostly interested in surprising letterforms and how they behave in a text. The limitations I invent for myself give me guidance, but also force me to live with the resulting imperfections. At the end, it is the imperfection I love most, not just in fonts.

Classification
Display

Styles
Regular

Release
2018

Contact
@martinlorenz
twopoints.net
@twopointsnet

Character overview on page 294

UNKNOWN
Lukas Haider, Alexander Raffl

Lukas and Alex met during their time at the Viennese graphic design studio GREAT. While working on concept sketches for a pitch, their research formed the aesthetic base of the typeface UNKNOWN. The name also originates from the topic of the pitch, in which the idea of "unknown territories" was explored in various visual forms. UNKNOWN is a contemporary display typeface consisting of 3 styles: RND (Rounded), PX (Pixelated) and MX (Mixed). These styles represent different approaches towards the same typeface, ranging from mechanically constructed to organically grown and a symbioses of the two, resulting in a mixture that could be described brutalism with the occasional soft curve. Although the typeface is based on a linear grid system, the overall appearance is still organic, giving each character enough freedom to have its own personality. UNKNOWN offers many alternate glyphs that can easily be substituted by using upper- or lowercase characters.

Classification
Pixel Grotesk

Styles
RND
PX
MX

Release
2020

Contact
lukashaider.com
@lkshdr
alexanderraffl.com
@alexanderraffl

Character overview on page 295

UNKNOWN   RND / PX / MX   2020

DUFOO:№26:$38☀Q?WHTA✳T£6MA¼🆎l™FA&CT#ROU↔¶D@[E]BGA☺♪+D,>§6L☼Rl%▣A!N☺UM=20G5VJSA▨
F40119K@S|3♫PJN€R⊕+⚅½¥O①‰F☻W©‡ZDM¢≈⊄@†⁖¢☯¢▲O@&«▽◑|🝙☺E5Q5≡⚹↑[>≈⚡⓶⊙F

Unpredictable Shadows
Colin Doerffler

Unpredictable Shadows was designed in 2018 as part of an artist contribution for a riso-graph-printed zine series published by CanCan Press (Mexico City). This contribution is titled "A snake eating its own tail inside a Rubik's cube on top of a Baudrillard book resting on a M.C. Escher staircase". What are letters today? The form urges itself in the foreground and the content falls back. Letters are cubistically deconstructed and separated from the claim, which is considered a construction of the phonetic alphabet. A recursive typography that regresses to its original: the pictorial form—iconoclasm by non-referenciality. A paradox in which the content can not change, only the form, but the form is the content. This leads to a change in structure and evolution of signs. Semantic content is caught up in its visuality: A snake eating its own tail. A visual tautology that leads iteratively to the question: Do letters have a future?—Does the future have letters?

Classification
Display

Styles
Regular

Release
2019

Contact
colindoerffler.com
@colindoerffler

Character overview on page 296

UNPREDICTABLE

SHADOWS

I DEDICATE

I   DEDICATE

MY WORK

MY   WORK

TO THOSE WHO

TO   THOSE   WHO

KNOW NOTHING

KNOW   NOTHING

ABOUT IT,

ABOUT   IT

WHO WILL NEVER

WHO   WILL   NEVER

KNOW ABOUT IT.

KNOW   ABOUT   IT

08:26

08   26

JULY 7, 2020

JULY   7,   2020

Vdushe Mono
Eleonora Šljanda

Vdushe Mono was created as a response to an assignment given by Sam de Groot. The task was to find a tool and create a typeface with it. The tool of my choosing was a transparent glass block. You can often find those in the bathroom interior. By using a flash light and pointing directly through the glass block, I found a fascinating grid which reflected on the wall. I documented this grid and used it to create the characters. By moving and flipping the grid around I achieved readable and good looking characters. Vdushe Mono characters could be treated as personalities. They are made to exist apart from the typeface as well, as autonomous elements. The characters can be used as tools to create illustrative elements or even exist as physical sculptures in the space. The Word "vdushe" has two meanings in Russian: "In the shower" and "in the soul".

Classification
Decorative

Styles
Regular

Release
2018

Contact
@eo407

Character overview on page 297

Voyant
Jake Dalton, Mason Peterson

Voyant is a loose jumble of characters drawn to focus on exaggerated curves and highlight the points where letters intersect with each other and themselves. The type was inspired by calligraphic serifs with an attempt to be reminiscent of both mechanical and more organic, botanical forms. The upper case maintains a mono-width to give all-caps a more mechanical feel while the characters in the sentence case vary more to allow for more diverse interactions between letterforms and to highlight the contrast and tension between sharp and more natural lines. Big thanks to Jake for lending a hand with Glyphs and a certain someone for the constant drive and inspiration, this one's for you. Make Well.

Classification
Serif

Styles
Regular

Release
2020

Contact
@howdyjake.exe
@mason_is_a_robot

Character overview on page 298

YOU
CAN   RUN
FROM
YOUR
PROBLEMS

ITS

A   GOOD
THING
TO
DO

VZWO ScytheSerif
Viktor Zumegen

VZWO ScytheSerif is designed and realized by Viktor Zumegen. It is a blackletter typeface that is highly constructed and "flowing" at the same time. The sweeping curves of the letters pick each other up and are continued by calligraphic elements. The result is a closed typeface with a strong emphasis on the horizontal lines through its impressive serifs. High contrast, extreme stroke endings, sharp curves as well as straight lines are dominating the typeface. The typeface often uses contextual alternates and has a stylistic set that makes it possible to create an "endless tape of type". VZWO ScytheSerif pursues the goal to turn type into an image.

Classification
Blackletter

Styles
Regular
Endless

Release
2018

Contact
@viktorzumegen

Character overview on page 299

TYPEFACE BY VIKTOR ZUMEGEN

VZHD SCYTHESERIF IS A BLACKLETTER TYPEFACE THAT IS HIGHLY CONSTRUCTED AND FLOWING AT THE SAME TIME. THE SWEEPING CURVES OF THE LETTERS PICK UP EACH OTHER AND ARE CONTINUED BY CALLIGRAPHIC ELEMENTS.

VZHD BLYTHE SERIF

...RIF IS A CLOSED TYPEFACE WITH A STRONG EMPHASIS ON THE HORIZONTAL LINES THROUGH THE IMPRESSIVE SE-RIF. HIGH CONTRAST, EXTREME STROKE ENDINGS, SHARP CURVES AS WELL AS STRAIGHT LINES ARE DOMINATING THE TYPEFACE. THE TYPEFACE OFTEN USES CONTEXTUAL ALTERNATES AND HAS A STYLISTIC SET THAT MAKES IT POSSIBLE TO CREATE AN ENDLESS TYPE OF TYPE. VZHD SCYTHESERIF PURSUES THE GOAL TO TURN TYPE INTO AN IMAGE.

Wabla
Daniel Stuhlpfarrer

Wabla is a combination of the words wabble and "Wappler"; it is an Austrian common word that describes a clumsy person. It is also used for people who pretend to be competent and capable, but in reality are completely incapable. Wabla is a decorative display typeface that shows its strength in large display sizes. It was developed for a magazine project where a modern translation of old initial letters was desired. Inspired by Jugendstil initial typefaces, such as the "Arnold Böcklin Initials" (1993, "Schriftgießerei Otto Weisert"), a more modern look was designed. Wabla comes in 5 Styles from Light to Black.

Classification
Display

Styles
Light
Regular
Medium
Bold
Black

Release
2019

Contact
danielstuhlpfarrer.com
@dnl_stu

Character overview on page 300

ABCD E A P D SSYF
F B J B K
S B C D A R . O B D U O O U
O L B . B E D L O L X
RANDBLATION OF OLD INITIAL LETTERS

Wired Serif
Nadine Wetzel

The typeface symbolizes captivity through the visual reference to a barbed wire fence. Through the connections between the letters, an individual character emerges with each use. The letters become a visual construct that speaks through contrasts in search of connection. In the process of drawing the typeface, it was important to create forms in which they would find themselves in a particular style and speak to each other. The first letters were sketched with a marker and after that with a spray can. With the provocative and specific shapes, Wired Serif will be very dominant in every use. The result is a character that has been influenced by his tools, taking an emotional position within a conceptual context.

Classification
Display

Styles
Regular

Release
2020

Contact
@nadine_wtzl

Character overview on page 301

IES ARE
BOUND
TOGETHER

WT Zaft
Jacob Jan Wise

Zaft is a weighty titling boldface, full of eccentricity and character. The face is distinctly heavy-handed in construction. Its strict systematic construction is arguably modernist, yet its fundamental architecture acknowledges the cultural relics of the Industrial Revolution; heavy slab-serifs and reverse-contrast. Apart from its ridged design, there is a playful rhythm and harmony to the negative space, allowing for delicate pockets of air to exist between the compact forms. This is further accentuated by Zaft's hairline letter spacing which helps focussing the eye on deviations within the glyph architecture without distraction. A unique feature worth noting is Zaft's use of contextual ligatures which form rounded connections between mirroring vertices. These gentle bridges are easy on the eye and add a vital elegance to its otherwise austere build. The face is equipped with a broad set of punctuation and an extended range of pan-European Latin characters.

Classification
Display

Styles
Titling Boldface
Slab Serif
P120Grit

Release
2019

Contact
wisetype.nl
@jacob.j.wise

Character overview on page 302

Grit Size

B&Q

Orbited

'14 rpm

Battery

2K:32

Magpie

(††—%×·)

Zephyr
Sophia Brinkgerd, Leonhard Laupichler

Zephyr is an expressive and delicate Italic Serif that was created collaboratively by Sophia Brinkgerd & Leonhard Laupichler for the Project Typescarf Season 3, which was initiated by Philipp Bulk. The typeface was made to suit the theme and mood of the scarf that carried the title "Heaven In A World So Cold". It plays with delicate but forceful italic strokes, sharp serifs and speaks an ornamental, light visual language that references the ambivalence of a daydream clashing with reality. When creating Zephyr, we were constantly reminded of a soft but forceful airflow, which is why we chose to revive one of the mystical Anemoi—the god embodied by the West Wind that is described in ancient greek mythology—through typography.

Classification
Serif

Styles
Italic

Release
2020

Contact
hey@sophiabrinkgerd.com
sophiabrinkgerd.com
@sophiabrinkgerd
leonhard@leonhardlaupichler.com
leonhardlaupichler.com
@leonhardlaupichler

Character overview on page 303

Acide Regular Slanted
Laura Csocsán

A B C D E F G H I J

K L M N O P Q R S T

U V W X Y Z

Data sheet on page 008

Airaz Regular
Javier Unknos

A B C D E F G H I J

K L M N O P Q R S T

U V W X Y Z

Data sheet on page 010

Aldiviva Autunno
Victor Gérard

A B C D E F G H I J
K L M N O P Q R S T
U V W X Y Z

a b c d e f g h i j
k l m n o p q r s t
u v w x y z

1 2 3 4 5 6 7 8 9 0

(! # § % & * ? @)

Data sheet on page 012

Alna Regular
Alff Rosine

𝒜 𝓑 𝒞 𝒟 𝒠 𝒡 𝒢 𝒣 𝒾 𝒿

𝒦 𝓛 𝓜 𝓝 𝒪 𝒫 𝒬 𝒦 𝒮 𝒯

𝒪 𝒱 𝒲 𝓍 𝒬 𝒵

Fatih Hardal

A B C D E F G H I J

K L M N O P Q R S T

U V W X Y Z

1 2 3 4 5 6 7 8 9 0

(! # $ % & ⁺ ? @)

Angels Racing Regular
Mārcis Lapiņš

Data sheet on page 018

Ara Regular
Felix Sandvoß

Data sheet on page 020

Archimède Regular
3,Quatorze

A B C D E F G H I J

K L M N O P Q R S T

U V W X Y Z

A B C D E F G H I J

K L M N O P Q R S T

U V W X Y Z

1 2 3 4 5 6 7 8 9 0

(! # $ % & * ? @)

Data sheet on page 022

ARP3 Regular
Ciarán Brandin

A B C D E F G H I J

K L M N O P Q R S T

U V W X Y Z

1 2 3 4 5 6 7 8 9 0

(! $ % &)

Data sheet on page 024

Arthemys Light
Morgane VanTorre

A B C D E F G H I J
K L M N O P Q R S T
U V W X Y Z

a b c d e f g h i j
k l m n o p q r s t
u v w x y z

1 2 3 4 5 6 7 8 9 0

Data sheet on page 026

Autark Regular
Stefanie Vogl

Data sheet on page 028

B—Sides Summer
Fabio Furlani

A B C D E F G H I J

K L M N O P Q R S T

U V W X Y Z

Data sheet on page 030

BRCKHRDT Regular
Gianluca Ciancaglini

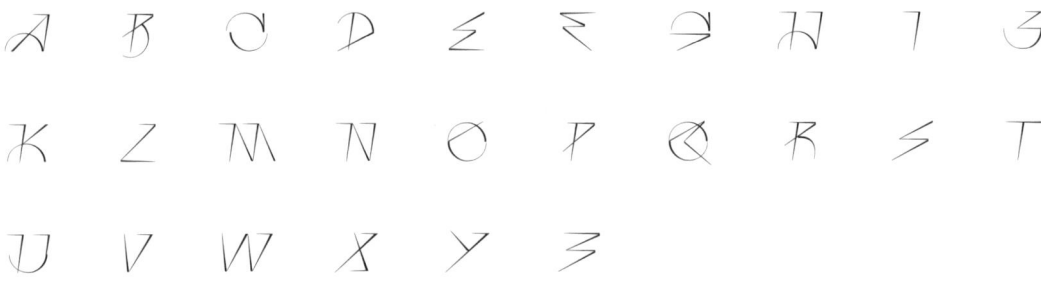

Data sheet on page 032

Mads-Emil Luplau, Bayonet Services

A B C D E F G H I J

K L M N O P Q R S T

U V W X Y Z

a b c d e f g h i j

k l m n o p q r s t

u v w x y z

1 2 3 4 5 6 7 8 9 0

(! # $ & ¤ ? @)

Data sheet on page 034

Chili Regular
Daniel Hermes

A B C D E F G H J ⊐

K L M N O P Q R S T

U U W X Y Z

Data sheet on page 036

Conztel Regular
Baptiste Bernazeau

A B C D E F G H I J

K L M N O P Q R S T

U V W X Y Z

a b c d e f g h i j

k l m n o p q r s t

u v w x y z

1 2 3 4 5 6 7 8 9 0

Data sheet on page 038

Dalmata Bold

Stefan Mader

a b c d e f g h i j

k l m n o p q r s t

u v w x y z

1 2 3 4 5 6 7 8 9 0

(! # $? @)

Data sheet on page 040

Dedale Regular
Awista Montagne

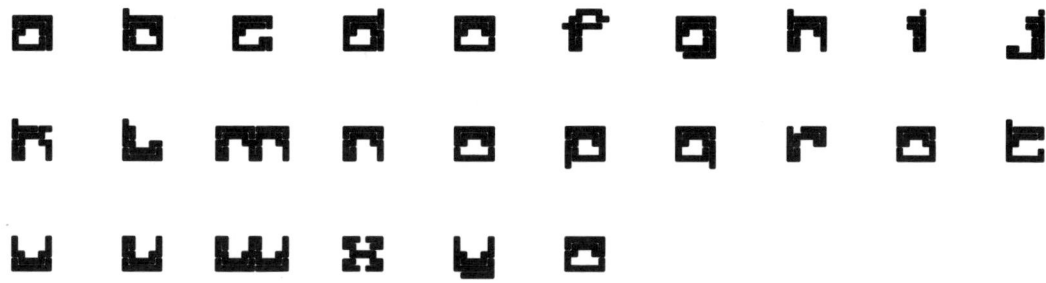

Data sheet on page 042

DG Sinusoide Regular
Davide Melotti

Data sheet on page 044

Eclect Regular
Gregory Page

a ɜ c ᴅ ɛ ꜰ ɢ ʜ ɪ ᴊ

ᴋ ʟ ᴍ ɴ ᴏ ᴘ ꞯ ʀ ꜱ ᴛ

ᴜ ᴠ ᴡ x ʏ ᴢ

Data sheet on page 046

Eryn Nouveau
Pauline Sesniac

A B C D E F G H I J
K L M N O P Q R S T
U V W X Y Z

Data sheet on page 048

Eyck Regular
Péter Polacsek

A B C D E F G H I J
K L M N O P Q R S T
U V W S Y Z

a b c d e f g h i j
k l m n o p q r s t
u v w s y z

Data sheet on page 050

Feeeels Fuzzy Regular
Jack Halten Fahnestock

A B C D E F G H I J

K L M N O P Q R S T

U V W X Y Z

a b c d e f g h i j

k l m n o p q r s t

u v w x y z

1 2 3 4 5 6 7 8 9 0

Data sheet on page 052

FF Duerer Light
Fabian Franz

A B C D E F G H I J
K L M N O P Q R S T
U V W X Y Z

Data sheet on page 054

Fluse Regular
Victor Pesotsky

A B C D E F G H I J
K L M N O P Q R S T
U V W X Y Z

a b c d e f g h i j
k l m n o p q r s t
u v w x y z

1 2 3 4 5 6 7 8 9 0

[! # $ % & * ? @]

Data sheet on page 056

Forsaken Display
Nicolas Terzian

Data sheet on page 058

Gallique Light
Emma Marichal

A B C D E F G H I J
K L M N O P Q R S T
U V W X Y Z

a b c d e f g h i j
k l m n o p q r s t
u v w x y z

Floriane Rousselot

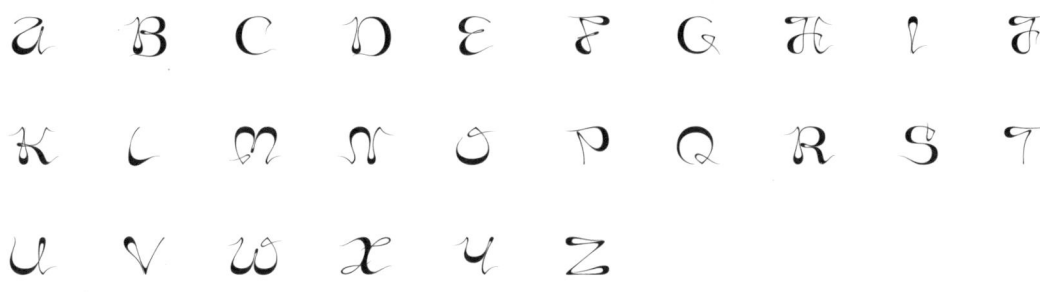

Data sheet on page 062

GlyphWorld Animal Soul
Leah Maldonado

Grief Regular
Alexandre Bassi

a b c d e f g h i j
k l m n o p q r s t
u v w x y z

 Data sheet on page 066

Hanol Light
Bouk RA

A B C D E F G H I J
K L M N O P Q R S T
U V W X Y Z

a b c d e f g h i j
k l m n o p q r s t
u v w x y z

1 2 3 4 5 6 7 8 9

Data sheet on page 068

Massimiliano Audretsch

A B C D E F G H I J
K L M N O P Q R S T
U V W X Y Z

a b c d e f g h i j
k l m n o p q r s t
u v w x y z

1 2 3 4 5 6 7 8 9 0
(! # % & * ?)

Data sheet on page 070

Hidde Grotesk Book
Matteo Bettini

A B C D E F G H I J

K L M N O P Q R S T

U V W X Y Z

a b c d e f g h i j

k l m n o p q r s t

u v w x y z

1 2 3 4 5 6 7 8 9 0

(! $ & * ? @)

Data sheet on page 072

Jugendstil Display
Robin Guillemin

A B C D E F G H I J

K L M N O P Q R S T

U V W X Y Z

a b c d e f g h i j

k l m n o p q r s t

u v w x y z

1 2 3 4 5 6 7 8 9 0

(! # $ % & * ? @)

Data sheet on page 074

Kasja Regular
Vivien Hoffmann

Data sheet on page 076

Katsu Grotesque Regular
Daniel Wenzel

A B C D Ɛ Ƒ Ǥ H I J

Ƙ L M N O P Q Ʀ S Ꞇ

Ц V W X Y Z

a b c d e f g ɦ i ị

k l м и o p q ɾ s t

ц v w x y z

1 2 3 4 5 6 7̶ 8 9 0

(! # $ % ⵦ * ⸮ @)

Data sheet on page 078

Kel-Var Display
Mathias Robert

A B C D E F G H I J

K L M N O P Q R S T

U V W X Y Z

Data sheet on page 080

Kéroïne Doux Extrême
Charlotte Rohde

A B C D E F G H I J

K L M N O P Q R S T

U V W X Y Z

a b c d e f g h i j

k l m n o p q r s t

u v w x y z

1 2 3 4 5 6 7 8 9 0

(! # $ & * ? @)

Data sheet on page 082

Kira Light
Mickaël Emile

A B C D E F G H I J
K L M N O P Q R S T
U V W X Y Z

a b c d e f g h i j
k l m n o p q r s t
u v w x y z

Data sheet on page 084

Koegi Regular
Zoé Abravanel

A B C D E F G H I J

K L M N O P Q R S T

U V W X Y Z

a b c d e f g h i j

k l m n o p q r s t

u v w x y z

Data sheet on page 086

Korosu Regular
Emilie Vizcano

A B C D E F G H I J
K L M N O P Q R S T
U V W X Y Z

a b c d e f g h i j
k l m n o p q r s t
u v w x y z

Data sheet on page 088

La Bretonnante Granit
Killian Maguet

A B C D E F G H I J
K L M N O P Q R S T
U V W X Y Z

a b c d e f g h i j
k l m n o p q r s t
u v w x y z

Data sheet on page 090

LeBug Regular
Jimmy Auger

A B C D E F G H I J

K L M N O P Q R S T

U V W X Y Z

Data sheet on page 092

Lily Regular
Antoine Brun

A B C D E F G H I J
K L M N O P Q R S T
U V W X Y Z

a b c d e f g h i j
k l m n o p q r s t
u v w x y z

1 2 3 4 5 6 7 8 9 0
(! # $ % & * ? @)

Data sheet on page 094

Lizard Regular
Robert Gutmann

Data sheet on page 096

Lobular Regular
Ariel Martín Pérez

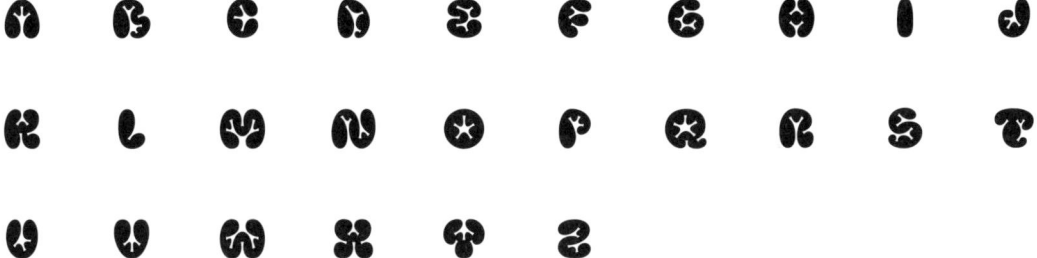

Data sheet on page 098

Macchia Regular
Brando Corradini

Data sheet on page 100

Magdalene Mono
Leah Maldonado

A B C D E F G H I J

K L M N O P Q R S T

U V W X Y Z

a b c d e f g h i j

k l m n o p q r s t

u v w x y z

Data sheet on page 102

Mars Light
Rémi Volclair

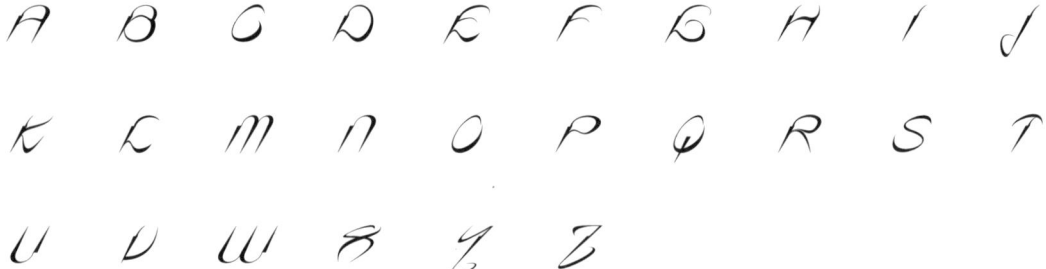

Data sheet on page 104

Monolog Irregular
Lennart Van den Bossche

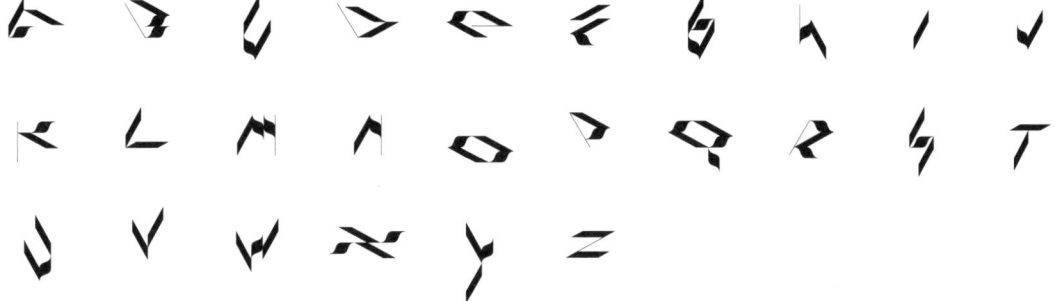

Data sheet on page 106

Monstrum Regular
Lorenza Liguori

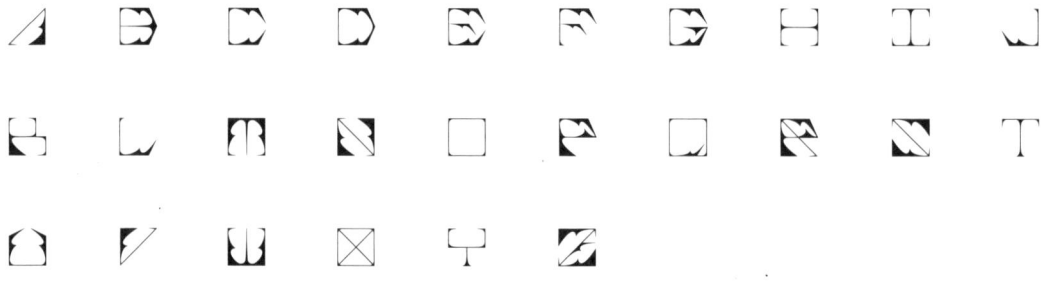

Data sheet on page 108

Mycela Regular
Peter Roeleveld

A B C D E F G H I J

K L M N O P Q R S T

U V W X Y Z

a b c d e f g h i j

k l m n o p q r s t

u v w x y z

(! # % & * ?)

Data sheet on page 110

Alex Ortiga

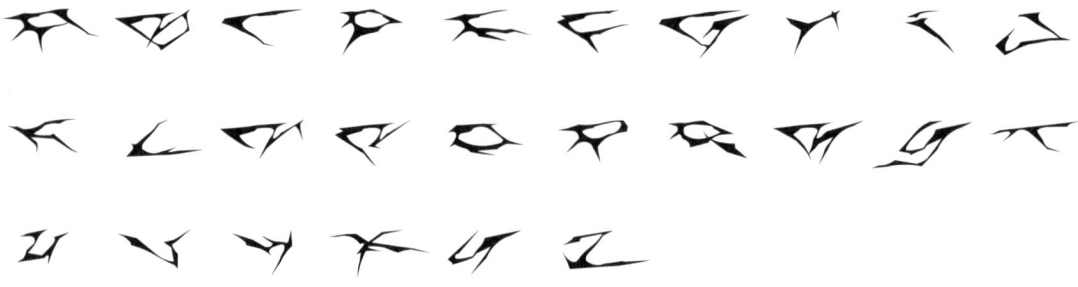

Data sheet on page 112

Mateo Broillet

A B C D E F G H I J
K L M N O P Q R S T
U V W X Y Z

a b c d e f g h i j
k l m n o p q r s t
u v w x y z

1 2 3 4 5 6 7 8 9 0
(! # $ % & * ? @)

Data sheet on page 114

Virgile Flores

A B C D E F G H I J
K L M N O P Q R S T
U V W X Y Z

a b c d e f g h i j
k l m n o p q r s t
u v w x y z

1 2 3 4 5 6 7 8 9 0
(! # $ % & * ? @)

Data sheet on page 116

New Diane Script Regular
Paul Bergès

A B C D E F G H I J

K L M N O P Q R S T

U V W X Y Z

a b c d e f g h i j

k l m n o p q r s t

u v w x y z

1 2 3 4 5 6 7 8 9 0

Data sheet on page 118

New Peace Regular
Panama Papers Office

A B C D E F G H I J

K L M N O P Q R S T

U V W X Y Z

Data sheet on page 120

Sophia Brinkgerd

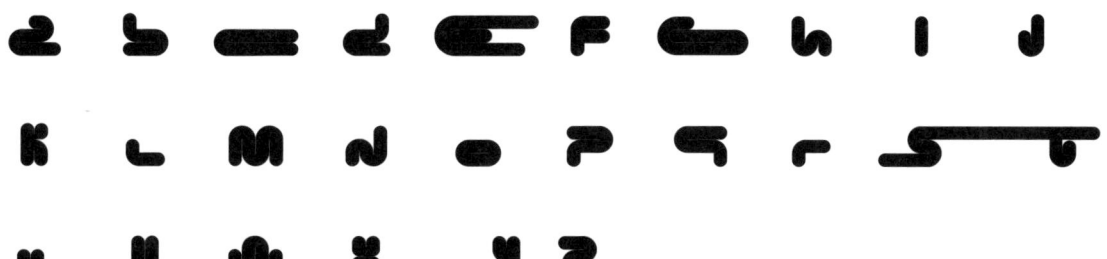

Data sheet on page 122

Raphaël De La Morinerie

a b c d e f g h i j

k l m n o p q r s t

u v w x y z

Data sheet on page 124

Noir Serif Regular
Lucas Hesse, Paul Schmidt, Malte Schwenker

A B C D E F G H I J

K L M N O P Q R S T

U V W X Y Z

a b c d e f g h i j

k l m n o p q r s t

u v w x y z

1 2 3 4 5 6 7 8 9 0

(! # % & ?)

Data sheet on page 126

Oliver Regular
Ishar Hawkins

a b c d e f g h i j

k l m n o p q r s t

u v w x y z

1 2 3 4 5 6 7 8 9 0

(! # $ % & * ? @)

Data sheet on page 128

Omelett Pose 2
Bedow Design

Data sheet on page 130

Once Again Extended
Han Gao

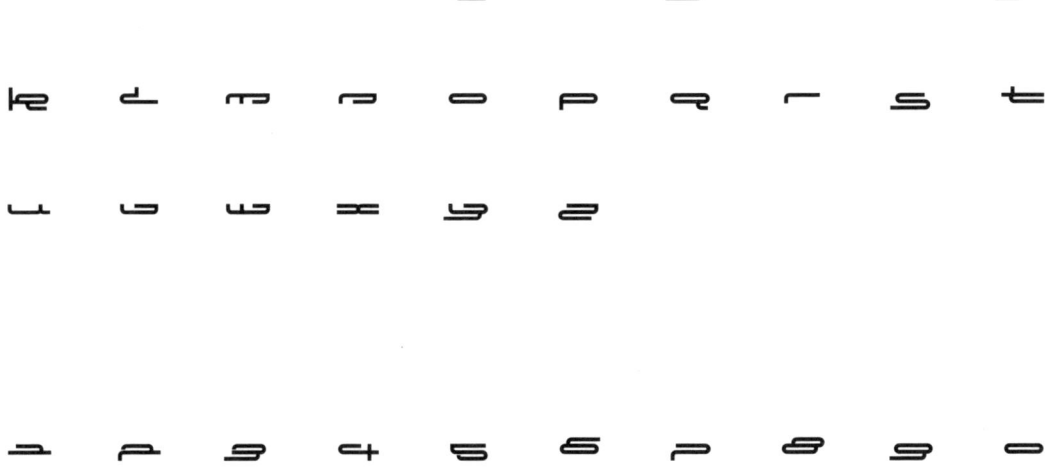

Data sheet on page 132

Ornamentum Regular
Hugo Jourdan

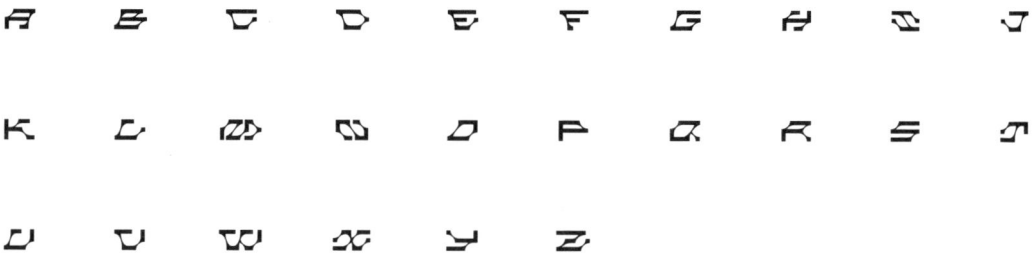

Data sheet on page 134

Pandemonium Regular
István Fazekas

A B C D E F G H I J

K L M N O P Q R S T

U V W X Y Z

Data sheet on page 136

Paradoxa Regular
Christos Georgatos

A B C D E F G H I J
K L M N O P Q R S T
U V W X Y Z

a b c d e f g h i j
k l m n o p q r s t
u v w x y z

1 2 3 4 5 6 7 8 9 0
(! # $ % & * ? @)

Data sheet on page 138

Pentex Inkspot
Sascha Bente

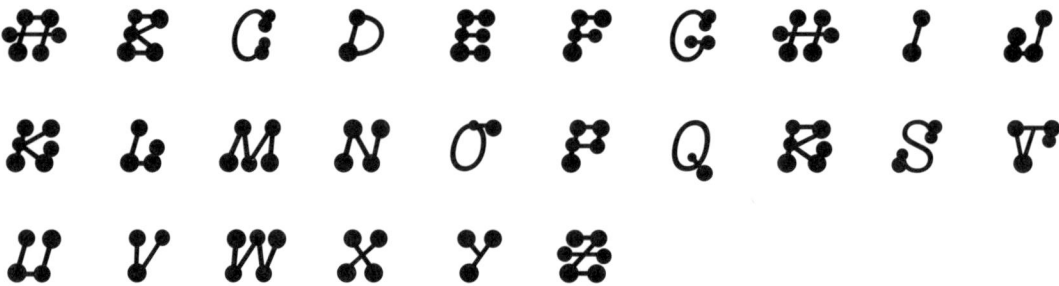

Data sheet on page 140

Elias Hanzer

A B C D E F G H I J

K L M N O P Q R S T

U V W X Y Z

a b c d e f g h i j

k l m n o p q r s t

u v w x y z

1 2 3 4 5 6 7 8 9 0

( ] # $ % & × ? @)

Data sheet on page 142

Poster Mono Regular
Lena Karoline Weber

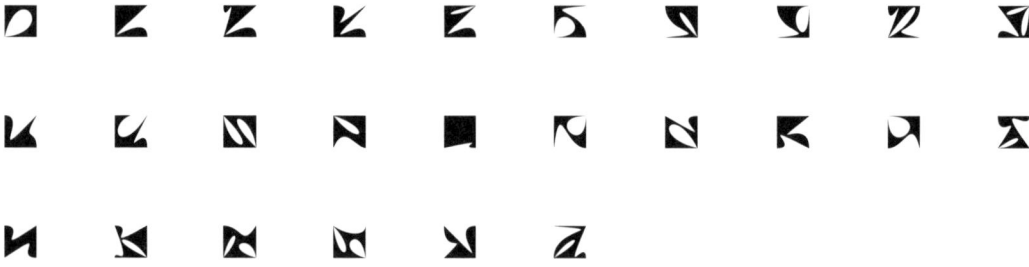

Data sheet on page 144

Protégé Regular
Paola Bombelli

A B C D E F G H I J
K L M N O P Q R S T
U V W X Y Z

a b c d e f g h i j
k l m n o p q r s t
u v w x y z

Data sheet on page 146

Rapido GP Regular
János Hunor Vári

A B C D E F G H I J

K L M N O P Q R S T

U V W X Y Z

a b c d e f g h i j

k l m n o p q r s t

u v w x y z

1 2 3 4 5 6 7 8 9 0

Data sheet on page 148

RED Regular
Frédéric Jaman, Vrints Kolsteren

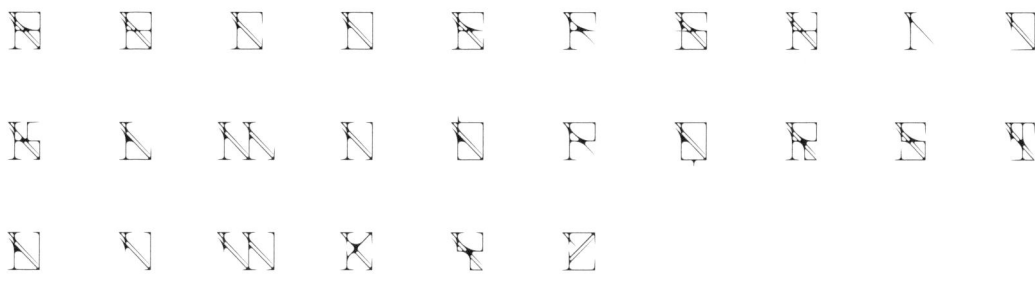

Data sheet on page 150

Renzo Univided
Robert Radziejewski

A B C D E F G H I J
K L M N O P Q R S T
U V W X Y Z

Data sheet on page 152

Romie Regular
Margot Lévêque

A B C D E F G H I J
K L M N O P Q R S T
U V W X Y Z

a b c d e f g h i j
k l m n o p q r s t
u v w x y z

1 2 3 4 5 6 7 8 9 0
(! # $ % & * ? @)

Data sheet on page 154

Rosdar Regular
Daan Rietbergen

Data sheet on page 156

Scotch Genovese Display
Scott Vander Zee

A B C D E F G H I J
K L M N O P Q R S T
U V W X Y Z

a b c d e f g h i j
k l m n o p q r s t
u v w x y z

1 2 3 4 5 6 7 8 9 0
(! # $ % & * ? @)

 Data sheet on page 158

Sentinel Regular
Eric Lish

A B C D E F G H I J

K L M N O P Q R S T

U V W X Y Z

a b c d e f g h i j

k l m n o p q r s t

u v w x y z

1 2 3 4 5 6 7 8 9 0

(! # $ % & * ? @)

Data sheet on page 160

Shinobi Regular
Kazuhiro Aihara

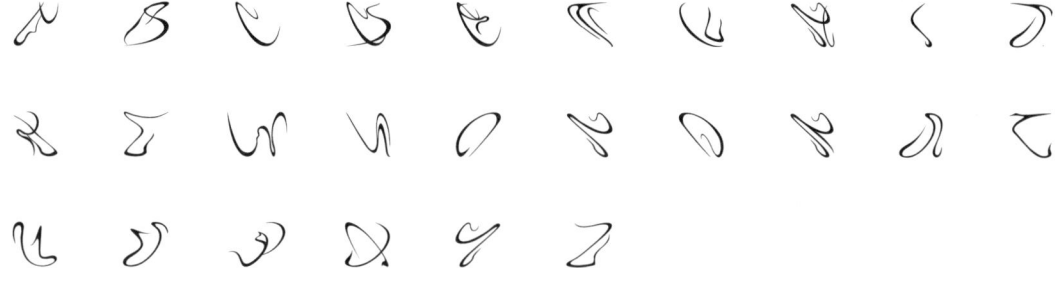

Data sheet on page 162

Shokoofeh Destruction
Leonhard Laupichler

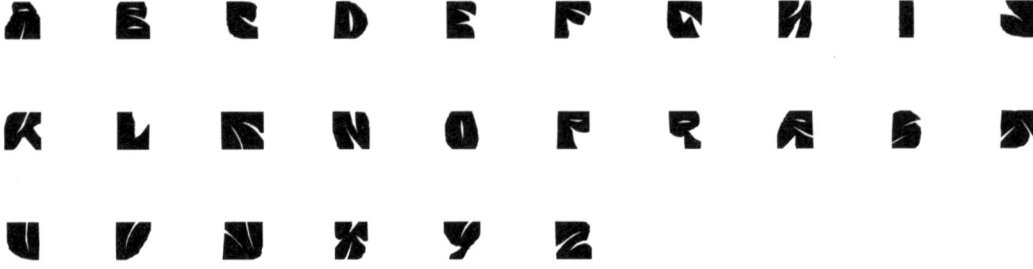

Data sheet on page 164

Sinistre Saint
Jules Durand

A B C D E F G H I J
K L M N O P Q R S T
U V W X Y Z

a b c d e f g h i j
k l m n o p q r s t
u v w x y z

1 2 3 4 5 6 7 8 9 0
(! $ % & * ? @)

Data sheet on page 166

Sissi Display Regular
Fabian Maier-Bode

A B C D E F G H I J
K L M N O P Q R S T
U V W X Y Z

a b c d e f g h i j
k l m n o p q r s t
u v w x y z

1 2 3 4 5 6 7 8 9 0

Data sheet on page 168

Sometimes Times Regular
Samuel Glen Hughes

A B C D E F G H I J
K L M N O P Q R S T
U V W X Y Z

a b c d e f g h i j
k l m n o p q r s t
u v w x y z

1 2 3 4 5 6 7 8 9 0
(! # $ % & * ? @)

Data sheet on page 170

SoundShape XP01 Curved
Giuseppe Tangaro

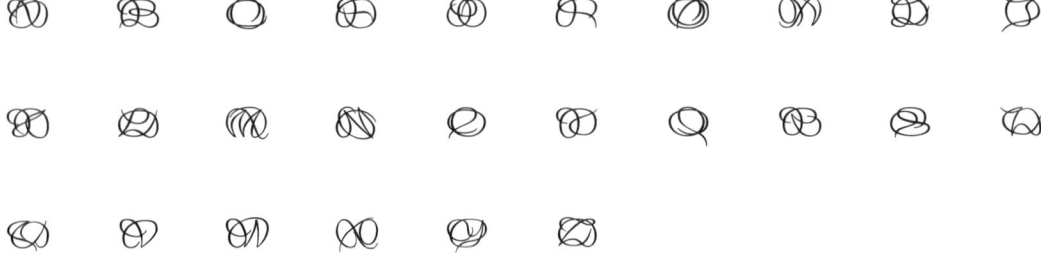

Data sheet on page 172

SpiritualRunes Regular
Sophia Krasomil

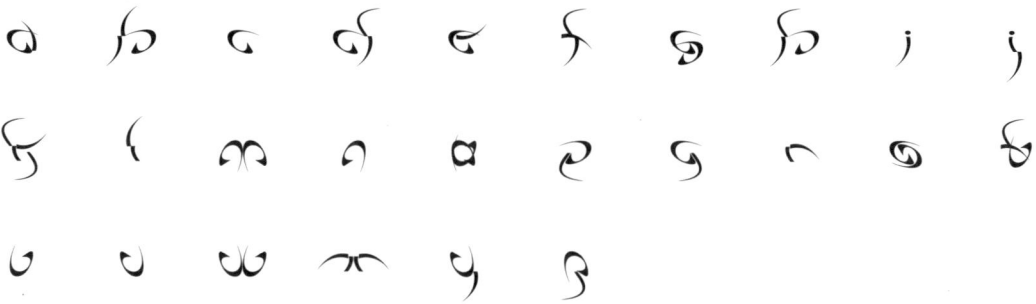

Data sheet on page 174

Splitter Regular
Arthur Schwarz

A B C D E F G H I J

K L M N O P Q R S T

U V W X Y Z

a b c d e f g h i j

k l m n o p q r s t

u v w x y z

Data sheet on page 176

Carolina Festa

A B C D E F G H I J
K L M N O P Q R S T
U V W X Y Z

a b c d e f g h i j
k l m n o p q r s t
u v w x y z

Techniquæ Antiqua Regular
Antonio D'Elisiis

A B C D E F G H I J
K L M N O P Q R S T
U V W X Y Z

a b c d e f g h i j
k l m n o p q r s t
u v w x y z

1 2 3 4 5 6 7 8 9 0

Data sheet on page 180

Pauline Le Pape

A B C D E F G H I J
K L M N O P Q R S T
U V W X Y Z

a b c d e f g h i j
k l m n o p q r s t
u v w x y z

1 2 3 4 5 6 7 8 9 0
(! # $ % & * ? @)

Data sheet on page 182

TpRawkost Regular

Dr. Martin Lorenz, TwoPoints.Net

A ᗷ < ▷ Ǝ Ξ Ϝ ⋖ ⊢ I ⌐

⊬ L M N ◇ Ꮲ Ǫ ꞧ Ƨ T

Ⴑ V W ✕ ⊻ Ƶ

1 Ƨ Ƶ 4 5 6 Ᏽ ⊠ ꓺ ◨

UNKNOWN MX
Lukas Haider, Alexander Raffl

A B C D E F G H I J

K L M N O P Q R S T

U V W X Y Z

1 2 3 4 5 6 7 8 9 0

(! # $ % & * ? @)

Data sheet on page 186

Unpredictable Shadows Regular
Colin Doerffler

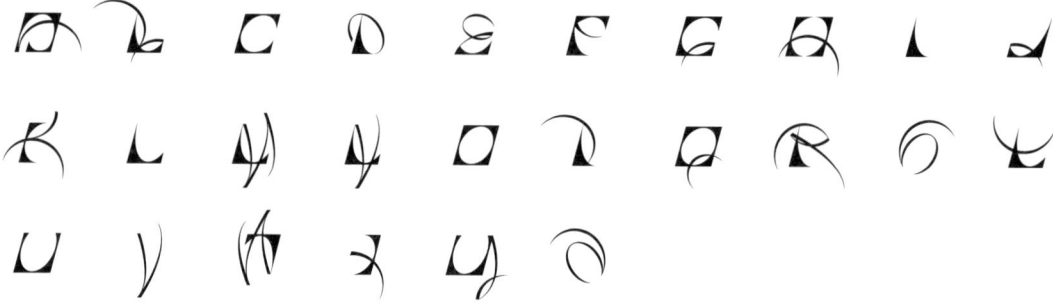

Data sheet on page 188

Vdushe Mono Regular
Eleonora Šljanda

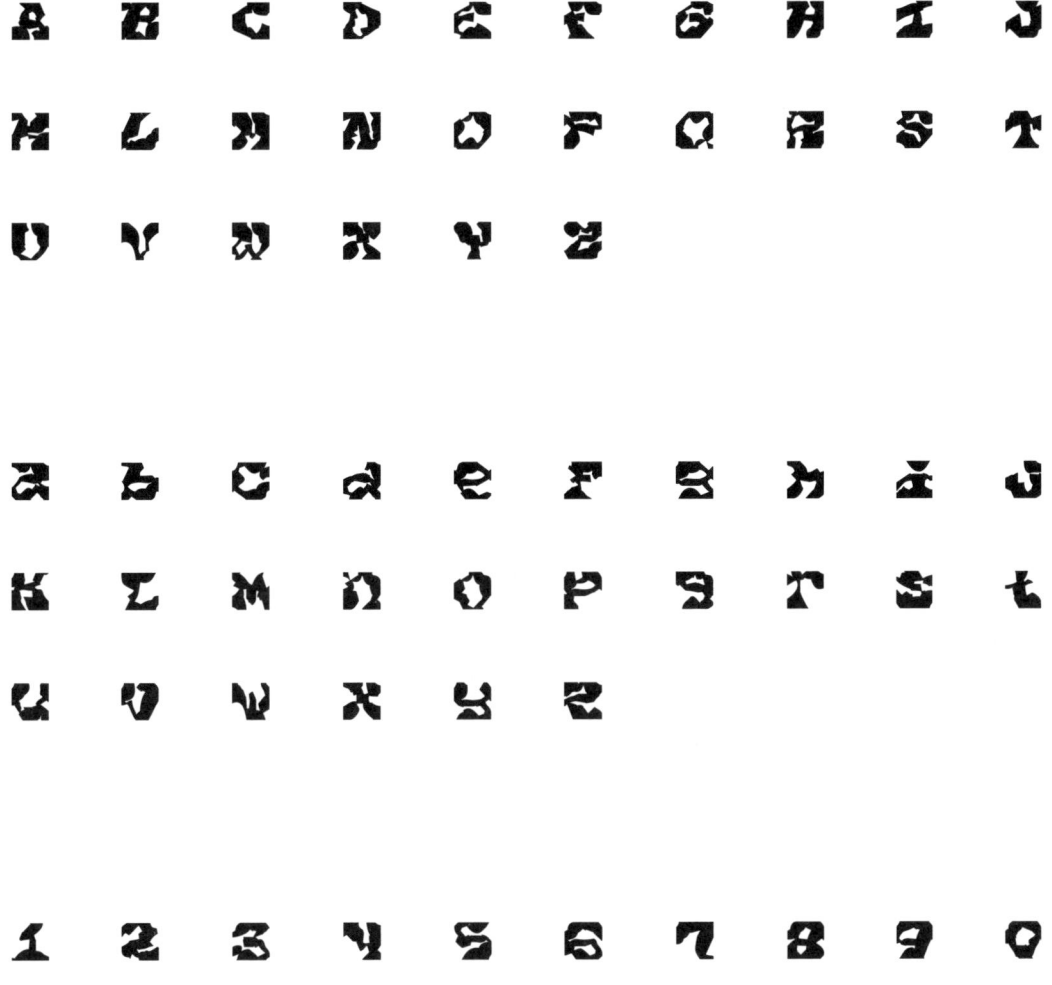

Data sheet on page 190

Voyant Regular
Jake Dalton, Mason Peterson

A B C D E F G H I J
K L M N O P Q R S T
U V W X Y Z

a b c d e f g h i j
k l m n o p q r s t
u v w x y z

Data sheet on page 192

VZWO ScytheSerif Regular
Viktor Zumegen

A B C D E F G H I J

K L M N O P Q R S T

U V W X Y Z

Daniel Stuhlpfarrer

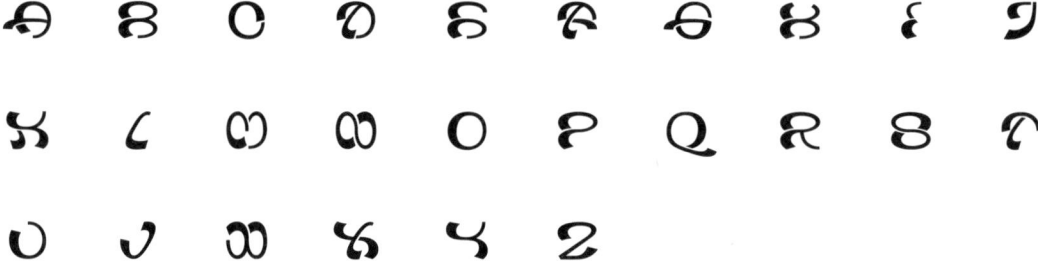

Data sheet on page 196

Wired Serif Regular
Nadine Wetzel

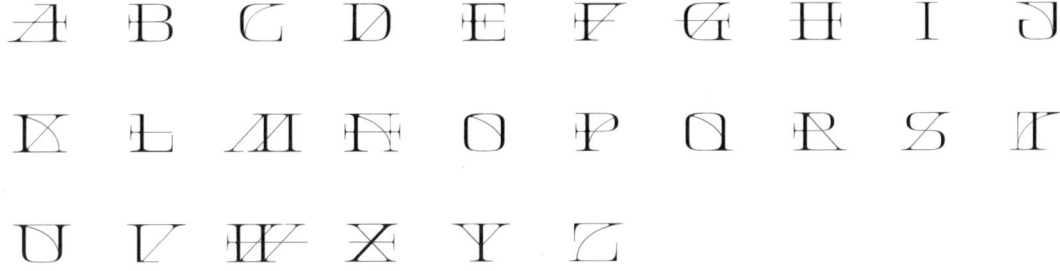

Data sheet on page 198

WT Zaft P120
Jacob Jan Wise

A B C D E F G H I J

K L M N O P Q R S T

U V W X Y Z

a b c d e f g h i j

k l m n o p q r s t

u v w x y z

1 2 3 4 5 6 7 8 9 0

(! # $ % & * ? @)

Data sheet on page 200

Zephyr Italic
Sophia Brinkgerd, Leonhard Laupichler

A B C D E F G H I J
K L M N O P Q R S T
U V W X Y Z

1 2 3 4 5 6 7 8 9 0

Data sheet on page 202

New Aesthetic 2
A Collection of Experimental and Independent Type Design

Editors
Leonhard Laupichler
Sophia Brinkgerd

Publisher
Sorry Press
www.sorry-press.com

Content Direction
Lukas Kubina

Design Direction
Wiegand von Hartmann
Moritz Wiegand, Sophie von Hartmann,
Maya Bendel

Production
Kopa

Printed in Lithuania
ISBN 978-3-9820440-3-3